Blender 4.3

User Guide

For Beginners and Professionals

A Comprehensive User Guide to Improved Animation, Sculpting
and Rendering for Smooth Production for Both Professionals
and Beginners.

Mathew Smit

Table of Contents

INTRODUCTION

Blender 4.3 is a free and open-source 3D creative tool is called Blender.

Blender allows you to generate 3D visualizations, including VFX shots, 3D animations, and still photos. Video editing is another skill you possess. Because of its fast development approach and unified pipeline, it is ideal for individuals and small studios.

Blender is a cross-platform program that may be used on Windows, Linux, and macOS. When compared to other 3D creative programs, it also has comparatively low memory and disk needs. To ensure a uniform experience on all supported platforms and hardware, its interface makes advantage of OpenGL.

Key Features

- A comprehensive suite of tools for creating 3D content, Blender includes modeling, rendering, animation and rigging, video editing, visual effects, compositing, texturing, and a variety of simulations.
- With an OpenGL GUI that is consistent across all main systems (and modifiable with Python scripts), it is cross-platform.
- Its superior 3D design allows for a quick and effective creation process.
- It has the active support of the community. An full list of sites may be found at blender.org/community.
- Without changing the system, it may be put into and launched from any directory.

CHAPTER 1: Getting Started

❖ Installing Blender 4.3

➤ Installing On Windows

Blender is easy to install on a Windows machine. With the help of this thorough instruction, you can install Blender 4.3 on your computer.

Process 1: Download Blender

- Visit Blender's official website: Go to Blender's official website.
- Click here to see the Downloads Page. Clicking the "Download" button will take you to the download page.
- Select the version of Windows: Blender may be used with both 32-bit and 64-bit versions of Windows. The 64-bit version is recommended for better performance and to take use of more RAM. Click the appropriate link to download   the   installation.

Process 2: Run the Installer

- Locate the Downloaded File: In your Downloads folder, look for the Blender installation file, usually named blender-4.3.0-windows-x64.msi or a similar one, once the download is complete.
- Launch the Installer: Double-click the installer file to begin the installation process.

Process 3: Install Blender 4.3

- The Setup Wizard will guide you through the installation process, so pay attention to it. Click "Next" to continue.
- Choose Installation place: You may choose to utilize the default installation directory or provide a different place. Click "Next" to proceed.
- Select Components: You may add "Blender Player" and shortcuts as extra components. Generally, leaving the default settings selected is appropriate. Click "Next."
- Install: Click the "Install" button to begin the installation. Blender will be installed on your PC through file copying by the installation. This might take a long time.
- Complete Installation: After the installation is complete, click "Finish" to end the Setup Wizard. You might be able to launch Blender at this very moment.

Process 4: Launch Blender

- To find the Blender shortcut after installation, search for "Blender" in the Windows search bar or navigate to the Start Menu.
- Launch Blender: Click the Blender icon to launch the application. When you initially use Blender, you may be prompted to select your preferred keymap (Blender's default, industry standard, etc.).

Process 5: Check the Installation

- After installing Blender, you may find the shortcut by searching for "Blender" in the Windows search bar or by selecting the Start Menu.
- Launch the Blender: To launch Blender, click the Blender icon. When using Blender for the first time, you may be prompted to select your preferred keymap (Blender's default, industry standard, etc.).

Troubleshooting

- Installation problems: If you're having trouble installing Blender 4.3, make sure your system meets the basic requirements and that you have the necessary permissions.
- If any Microsoft Visual C++ Redistributables are missing, Blender could require them. If asked, allow the installer to download and install these parts.
- Graphics Drivers: Make sure your graphics drivers are up to date to avoid performance issues or graphical defects.

  ▪ **System Requirement For Windows**

	Recommended	*Minimum*
OS	Windows 10/ Windows 11	Windows 8.1 (64-bit)
CPU	8 cores	4 cores that Support SSE4.3
RAM	32 GB	8GB
GPU	8 GB VRAM	2GB VRAM with OpenGL 4.3

  ▪ **Installing on macOS**

STEP 1: Download Blender 4.3

- Installation problems: If you're having trouble installing Blender 4.3, make sure your system meets the basic requirements and that you have the necessary permissions.

- If any Microsoft Visual C++ Redistributables are missing, Blender could require them. If asked, allow the installer to download and install these parts.
- Graphics Drivers: Make sure your graphics drivers are up to date to avoid performance issues or graphical defects.

STEP 2: Open the Installer

- Locate the Downloaded File: After the download is complete, you should be able to find the.dmg file in your Downloads folder. You should name the file blender-4.3.0-macOS.dmg.
- Open the DMG file. Double-clicking the.dmg file will open it. This will cause the Blender application icon to open in a new window and the disk image to mount.

STEP 3: Install Blender 4.3

- Drag Blender to Applications: Drag the Blender icon into the window that appears to move it to the Applications folder shortcut. Blender may be accessed like any other installed software by copying it to your Applications folder.
- Close the Installer Window: After the copy is complete, you can either drag the disk image to the Trash or use the "Eject" option in the Finder to get rid of it from the installer.

STEP 4: Launch Blender 4.3

- To unlock Blender, navigate to your Applications folder and choose Blender. Double-clicking will launch Blender.
- Disregard Security Warnings: When you initially use Blender, it can indicate that it was downloaded from the

internet. This is a standard macOS security feature. Click "Open" to confirm that you want to launch the application.

- Select Keymap (Optional): When you initially launch Blender, it could offer you to choose a keymap (Blender's default, industry standard, etc.). Make a decision and go forward.

STEP 5: Verify Installation

- Check Blender Version: You may use the top menu bar to navigate to Blender > About Blender or the splash screen that appears when the program first launches to confirm the installed version of Blender.
- Examine the User Interface: Become acquainted with Blender's settings and user interface. You may customize Blender to fit your workflow by changing its options.

Troubleshooting

- Permissions Problems: Verify that you have administrator rights on your Mac in case you run into permission problems during installing.
- Protector of the Gates Caution: Blender may not open if macOS Gatekeeper is unable to validate the developer. In such circumstances, choose "Open Anyway" for Blender under System Preferences > Security & Privacy > General.
- Performance and Graphics: To prevent graphical hiccups or performance problems, make sure your macOS and graphics drivers are up to date.

- **System Requirement For macOS**

	Recommended	Minimum
OS	macOS 14 (Sonoma)	macOS 11.2 (Big Sur)
CPU	Apple Silicon	Apple Silicon/ Intel
RAM	32 GB	8 GB
GPU		GPU with Metal 2.2

- **Installing on Linux**

Depending on the distribution you're running, there are subtle differences in how to install Blender on a Linux machine. Nonetheless, installing the program and downloading it are the standard procedures. This is a step-by-step tutorial that walks you through installing Blender 4.3 on a Linux computer, with special instructions for Fedora and Ubuntu.

STEP 1: Download Blender

- Go to the Blender website: Go to Blender's official website.
- Visit the page for downloads: To get to the download page, click the "Download" button.
- Choose the Linux Version: There is a Linux version of Blender available. To get the tarball (.tar.xz file), click the Linux link.

STEP 2: Extract the Tarball

- Find the file you downloaded: The .tar.xz file you downloaded can be found in your browser's file save location or in the Downloads folder.
- Launch the Terminal: To extract the tarball, you can use the terminal or a graphical file manager. This is how you use the terminal to accomplish it:
  - Go to the directory where the downloaded file is located:
    cd ~/Downloads
  - Extract the tarball:
    tar -xf blender-4.3.0-linux-x64.tar.xz

Blender will be extracted by running this command into a directory called blender-4.3.0-linux-x64; the precise name may differ depending on the version.

STEP 3: Lunching Blender 4.3

1. Go to Blender's Directory by clicking here. Make a directory change in Blender:
   cd blender-4.3.0-linux-x64
2. Start the Blender: Launch the Blender application:
   ./blender

You may now launch Blender and start utilizing the program.

STEP 4: Creating a Desktop Shortcut (Optional)

You may construct a desktop shortcut or launcher to make it simpler to open Blender:

1. Make a file for desktop entry: Launch a text editor and make a new file with the contents listed below:
   [Desktop Entry]
   Name=Blender

Comment=Blender 4.3
Exec=/path/to/blender-4.3.0-linux-x64/blender
Icon=/path/to/blender-4.3.0-linux-x64/blender.svg
Terminal=false
Type=Application
Categories=Graphics;3DGraphics;

Replace /path/to/blender-4.3.0-linux-x64/ with the actual path to your Blender directory.

2. Save the File: Save the file with a .desktop extension, for example, blender.desktop.
3. Turn on the file's execution: Declare a file executable: *chmod +x blender.desktop*
4. Transfer the File to the Applications Folder: Transfer the desktop icon to the relevant directory: *mv blender.desktop ~/.local/share/applications/*

STEP 5: Updating Blender

You may update Blender by downloading the most recent tarball, extracting it, and then doing the setup and extraction instructions again when a new version becomes available.

Troubleshooting

- Dependencies: Make sure your system has the necessary components, such as the relevant OpenGL and other library versions. Any missing requirements may frequently be installed using your package manager.
- Permissions: If you encounter permission issues, you may need to utilize sudo to carry out specific operations.

- Graphics Drivers: Make sure your graphics drivers are up to date to avoid performance issues or graphical defects.

CHAPTER 2: Editors

❖ **Startup Scene**

The startup scene appears in the 3D Viewport after the splash screen closes (assuming no other blend-file was loaded). The opening scene can be altered.

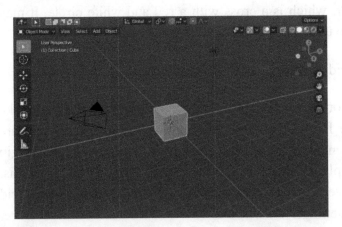

- **Elements**

● Cube

A mesh object is the gray cube in the scene's center. It is selected as shown by its orange outline. Its exact location is shown by the orange dot at the center, which is called its Origin.

● Brightness

The light source that illuminates the cube is the collection of concentric black rings.

● Snapshot

The camera, which serves as the rendering point of view, is represented by the pyramid with the large triangle perched over it.

- 3D Pointer

The location of newly inserted items is shown by the 3D pointer, which is a cross with a red and white circle. It may also be used as a pivot point for transformations.

- Grid Surface

The world's zero height is shown by the gray lines that make up the floor. The axes of the global coordinate system are represented by the red and green lines. They meet at the origin of the planet, which is also the location of the Cube's genesis. The overlays viewport popover is where you find the Grid Floor settings.

- Text Details

For more information, see Viewport Overlays. Various bits of information are displayed in the upper left corner of the viewport.

❖ **Object Mode**

Modes let you alter several features of an object. You can position, rotate, and scale them in Object Mode; you can alter their geometry in Edit Mode; you can pose them in Pose Mode, and so on.

The 3D Viewport header's Mode selection can be used to alter the mode that is currently in use. The type of item determines the accessible modes. Below is a list of everything on it.

In addition to using the picker, you may also quickly access items by pressing Ctrl-Tab, which displays a pie menu around the cursor. (This shortcut will alternate between item Mode and Pose Mode if the chosen item is a Armature.)

Toggle Editing Mode on items that support it by pressing Tab.

In Blender, modes may impact several aspects:

- Every mode displays a different collection of menus and tools by altering the header and Toolbar. Thus, it also has an impact on the keyboard shortcuts that are available.
- Modes allow you to alter the viewport's appearance entirely. For instance, the object's vertex weights, which are ordinarily hidden, will be seen by shading it while using the Weight Paint mode.
- Editors might be impacted by modes. For instance, the 3D Viewport must be in Edit Mode in order to utilize the UV Editor. There are other buttons and panels in the Properties editor that are limited to particular modes of operation.

- **Object Mode List**

Icon	Name	Details
	Object Mode	The standard mode, appropriate for all kinds of objects. enables duplicating objects, adjusting scale, rotation, and location, among other features.
	Edit Mode	A mode for manipulating the form of an object (e.g., points/strokes for Grease Pencil, control points for curves/surfaces, vertices/edges/faces for meshes, etc.).
	Sculpt Mode	Gives users another set of tools to change an object's form (but just for meshes).
	Vertex Paint Mode	An exclusive mode for meshes that lets you "paint" or customize the colors of its vertex sets.
	Weight Paint Mode	A mode limited to mesh that is used for vertex group weighting.
	Texture Paint Mode	A mesh-only mode that lets you use the 3D Viewport to paint a texture directly onto the object.
	Particle Edit Mode	An editable system (hair) can benefit from this mesh-only mode for particle systems.

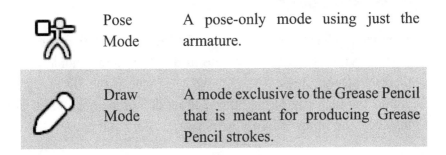

	Pose Mode	A pose-only mode using just the armature.
	Draw Mode	A mode exclusive to the Grease Pencil that is meant for producing Grease Pencil strokes.

- **Multi-Object Editing**

Because many objects may be in Edit Mode and Pose Mode at once, working with numerous objects is considerably easier than it is in the previous description.

There are two approaches to doing this:

- To enter the mode if you haven't already, just pick every object and press enter.
- Once you're in the mode, you may use Ctrl-LMB to choose more items by clicking on the outliner's dot. The process is the same for removing things from the mode.

A few noteworthy points are:

- Only the details (shape keys, UV maps, etc.) of the current item will ever be displayed in the Properties editor; not all of the chosen objects will.
- Any element within an object becomes the active element when it is selected.
- The modifications you may make are restricted. For instance, you are unable to construct an edge that joins the vertices of many objects.

❖ Navigating

You need to be able to adjust both the viewing direction and your point of view in order to operate in the three-dimensional realm that Blender employs. Although we will focus on the 3D Viewport editor, the majority of the other editors do comparable tasks. For instance, the Image editor allows you to zoom and pan.

▪ Navigation Gizmo

The editor's upper right corner is where you'll find the navigation device.

The view's current orientation is displayed via the Orbit gadget at the top. It will circle the screen if you drag it with LMB. Any axis label may be clicked to align the view with that axis. The other side of the same axis is selected by clicking on it once more.

▪ Walk or Fly Navigation

Occasionally, the built-in navigation controls might be restrictive, particularly in expansive settings like architectural models. Instead of circling around a central perspective in certain situations, it could be better to employ first-person controls, where you can gaze around while "standing" in one spot.

Flying and Walking are two such other navigation techniques that Blender provides. Either approach may be started from the View ▸ Navigation menu. You may also use Shift + Accent Grave to start your favorite (set in the Preferences).

Typical Fly/Walk use cases are as follows:

- Getting Around

This can be an efficient technique to move about a big scene.

- Setting up a camera

Activated from a Numpad0 camera view, the camera moves with you.

- capturing the motion of the camera

By going into camera view, turning on Auto Keying in the Timeline, playing back animations, and then turning on Fly/Walk navigation, you may capture the route you walk. The route will be captured as keyframes from the camera, which may be utilized for rendering later.

Fly/Walk navigation cannot be managed while animation playback is in progress, therefore in order to halt playback once you've finished recording, you must first use LMB to quit the navigation.

- **Orthographic or Perspective**

This operator modifies the viewport camera's projection. Two distinct projection formats are supported by every 3D Viewport.

Perspective vision, in which far-off things look smaller, is accustomed to our eyes. Because objects with orthographic projection maintain their same size at all distances, it may first look a little strange. It feels as though you are looking at the sight from a very far distance. However, because orthographic seeing offers a more "technical" perspective on the image, it may be highly helpful in modeling and judging proportions.

- **Local View**

All of the scene's 3D objects are visible in global view. The selected item or objects are isolated in local view, making them the only ones visible in the viewer. This helps to speed up viewport performance in scenes with a lot of items or to work on things that are hidden by other objects. Since local view is contextual, it may be adjusted for each 3D Viewport.

By choosing the choice from the View menu or by using the Numpad-Slash shortcut, you may switch between the Global and Local Views.

❖ **3D Cursor**

A point in space with both a position and a rotation is called a 3D cursor. It serves several different functions. It may be used, for instance, to manually place and orient the transform device (see Pivot Point and Transform Orientation) and define the locations of newly added items. A few tools additionally make use of the Cursor, such Bend.

- **Placement**

The 3D Cursor may be positioned in many ways.

The most versatile tool is the Cursor tool. To position the 3D Cursor, just choose it from the Toolbar and use LMB to click on a point in the scene. You may select the orientation of the tool in the tool settings. By default, it aligns with the view orientation, but you can alternatively align it with the transform orientation or the surface normal of a piece of geometry.

As an alternative, you may choose any tool and hit Shift + RMB. The 3D Cursor in this instance will always be oriented in line with the view.

You should employ two orthogonal, perpendicular 3D viewports for accuracy, which can be any combination of side Numpad3, front Numpad1, and top Numpad7. In this manner, you may decide on the depth in one view and manage the location along two axes in another.

The depth for the geometry beneath the cursor is utilized by default. The Pointer Surface Project toggle in the Settings may be used to deactivate this.

❖ **Display**

▪ **Object Type Visibility**

You may adjust which item kinds are visible and selectable using this popover. For instance, you only need to click once to turn off all of the lights in the scene.

This just affects the 3D Viewport that is open at the moment. Certain object types that are designated as unselect able remain selectable in other viewports, such as the Outliner.

▪ **Object Gizmos**

In the 3D Viewport, Object Gizmos provide mouse-controlled translation, rotation, and scaling. Even though they are referred to as "object" gizmos in the popover, mesh vertices and other transformable components are also covered by them.

Every surgery has its own gadget. You can use each gadget alone or in conjunction with the others.

Three color-coded axes are included on every gadget: X (red), Y (green), and Z (blue). LMB allows you to translate along an axis by dragging it. Additionally, the Move and Scale devices have tiny colored squares that allow for simultaneous transformation along two axes.

There are several modifier keys available:

- Toggle snapping and enable coarse-acceleration rotation and scaling by holding down the Ctrl key at any moment.
- To do the reverse of what is described above, hold Shift after hitting LMB. This will "slow down" the transformation in relation to mouse movement, enabling more precise changes.
- To execute the transformation in the plane perpendicular to the clicked axis, hold Shift before hitting LMB. Refer to Aircraft Locking.

The following options are available for object gizmos in the Gizmos popover:

- Orientation
  The device's orientation to use. Using the viewport's transform orientation is what is meant by default. The other choices take precedence.
- Move
  To control the location, show the device. The viewing plane may be moved freely by dragging the little white circle.
- Rotate

To regulate the rotation, show the device. Rotating around the viewing direction is possible by dragging the huge white circle. Trackball rotation is accomplished by dragging the translucent white disc (seen only when hovering above the device) inside that circle.

- Measurement
  Display the device to operate the scale. Using all three axes, drag the region between the tiny and big white circles scales.

  - **Viewport Shading**

Blender has many shading modes to assist with various tasks. For instance, rendered shading works well for lighting setup, whereas solid shading works better for modeling.

The drop-down button opens a popover with more settings explained below, and the radio buttons allow you to adjust the shading mode.

To change the shading mode, press Z to bring up a pie menu. To transition between the current shading mode and Wireframe, press Shift-Z.

  ❖ **Viewport Rendering**

Quick preview renderings can be produced using viewport rendering, as opposed to conventional renders, which originate from the active camera.

Viewport Render may be used to render animations as well as pictures.

A comparison of the final render produced using the Cycles Renderer and the Viewport render can be seen below.

- **Settings**

Viewport Render mostly makes use of the viewport's current parameters. The render engine attributes, which are where the view is rendered, contain some parameters.

Workbench render parameters are used in Solid mode; EEVEE render settings are used in Material Preview mode.

Furthermore, the following output options are also used:

- Resolution
- Aspect
- Path of output
- Format for files

- **Rendering**

Rendering from the active view is what happens when you activate Viewport Render. This implies that a virtual camera is utilized to match the current viewpoint if you are not in an active camera view. Use Numpad0 to access the active camera view in order to obtain an image from the camera's point of view.

Use Esc to stop it, just like you would with any other render.

- Rendering a Motionless Picture

A still image may be rendered using 3D Viewport. View ▸ Viewport Render a picture.

- Rendering an Animation

3D Viewport may be used to render an animation. Viewport Render Animation is available.

❖ **Image Editing**

▪ **Overlay**

The overlays that appear over photographs may be customized using the Overlays pop-over. There is a button in the header to disable the Image Editor's overlays altogether. Additionally, this option toggles whether UDIM tile information is shown.

Depending on the Image Editor mode, different choices are displayed in the pop-over. There are the following possible overlay categories:

● Geometry

UVs of Display Texture Paint

Show the UVs of the current item. For the UVs to be visible, the current object must be in either Texture Paint Mode or Edit Mode and the Image Editor must be in Paint mode.

● Picture

Display Metadata

Shows the selected render result's information. To modify the metadata to be included, view the Metadata panel on the Output tab.

CHAPTER 3: User Interface

❖ **Splash Screen**

Blender displays a splash screen in the middle of the window when it first launches. It offers the ability to start fresh projects or open old ones. A more thorough explanation is provided below.

To quit the splash screen and start a new project, click anywhere on it (but still inside the Blender window) or press Esc. When the splash screen disappears, the default screen will appear. To display the splash screen again, click the Blender icon in the Topbar and select Splash Screen.

❖ **Top Bar**

Blender 4.3's Topbar is a crucial component of the user interface, offering instant access to key features and configuration options. It extends over the top of the Blender window and has a number of tools and menus to help with productive working. Below is a summary of the Topbar's primary elements and functionalities:

- **Main Menus**

File Edit Render Window Help

- **File:** You may save and export your work using this menu, as well as create new files and open old ones. It also has settings for importing and exporting different formats, accessing user preferences and add-ons, and connecting and appending data from other Blender files.
- Edit: With the tools under the Edit menu, you can copy and paste, undo and redo actions, and access settings. Among other things, it offers the ability to alter input configurations and themes.
- Generate: Using this option, you can select whether to generate your scene as an animation or as an image. You may also access the render view and render settings.
- Window: Here, you configure Blender's window settings, including navigating between workspace and full-screen modes.
- Help: Links to the Blender manual, community forums, and other resources are available through the Help menu. It's a helpful tool for finding assistance.

- **Workspace Tabs**

The workspace menus have tabs just beneath them. You may transition between many workspaces using these tabs, each one designed for a particular purpose, such as UV editing, shading, animation, modeling, sculpting, rendering, compositing, and scripting. Workspaces can be added, changed, or removed as needed.

- **Tool Settings**

Options unique to the tool that is now selected are available in the Tool Settings panel, which is often located on the right side of the Topbar. With parameters and settings that may be changed for exact control over your activities, this panel adjusts itself based on the active tool. For instance, the Tool Settings allow you to easily adjust the brush's size, strength, and falloff.

- **Scene Information And Settings**

- Scene Selection: This feature lets you move between scenes in a single Blender project.
- View Layer: You may utilize many view layers to arrange and render different portions of your scene independently.
- Select from a variety of render engines, such as Cycles, Eevee, and others. Performance and rendering quality are impacted by this parameter.
- Access and modify camera and render settings quickly, including the current camera for rendering.

- **Contextual Menus and Operators**

The Topbar may show other menus and operators related to the current task, depending on the mode and context. For example, you could see brush-specific choices in Sculpt Mode and playback and keyframing options in Animation Mode.

- **Quick Search and Navigation**

A search bar is frequently included in the Topbar to aid in locating tools, commands, and settings fast. When it comes to accessing functions without having to go through several menus, this feature is really helpful.

- **Customization and Accessibility**

The Topbar and the Blender interface are both quite customizable. To suit your workflow, you may reorder pieces, conceal or expose particular menus, and change the layout. Whether you're interested in modeling, animation, or any other area of 3D development, Blender's customizable interface allows you to tailor it to your requirements.

❖ **Regions**

In Blender, each Editor is separated into regions. Smaller organizing components, such as tabs and panels with buttons, controls, and widgets positioned inside of them, can be included into regions.

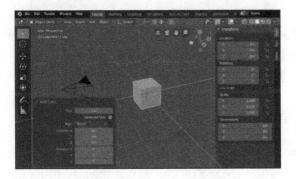

➢ **Main Region**

There is always at least one visible zone. It is the most noticeable area of the editor and is referred to as the Main section.

The primary region and the availability of supplementary areas vary between editors due to their distinct purposes. See the Editors chapter for further information on each editor.

➢ Header

A header is a narrow strip of horizontal text that appears at the top or bottom of a section. Every editor has a header that houses frequently used tools and menus. Depending on the type of editor, the item and mode selected, menus and buttons will alter.

➢ Toolbar

Interactive tools are located in the Toolbar, which is located on the left side of the editing area. T changes the Toolbar's visibility on and off.

➢ Tool Settings

A horizontal bar with the tool's settings now chosen that sits at the top or bottom of the editor, resembling the header. It has the same context menu functionality as the header, allowing for movement and hiding.

➢ Adjust Last Operation

An operator can be adjusted after it has been executed by using the Adjust Last Operation area. You can adjust the size of a cube, for instance, by using this region if it was just introduced.

➢ Side Bar

Panels with options for both the editor and its own objects may be found in the Sidebar, which is located on the right side of the editor area. N changes the Sidebar's visibility on and off.

> **Footer**

Certain editors have a bar that shows information about the active tool or operator, for example, at the top or bottom of the editor area.

- **Arranging**

Scrolling

Using the MMB, a section may be dragged vertically or horizontally to scroll. The Wheel may also be used to scroll a region without a zoom level by dragging it with the mouse while it is in the hover state.

Certain areas—animation timelines, for example—have scrollbars with extra control points to change the region's vertical or horizontal range. The ends of these unique scrollbars will include extra widgets, as seen in the picture below:

With this, you may adjust the range to display a greater or lesser detail in the given screen area. To change the range that is displayed, just drag one of the dots. By dragging in the editor with Ctrl + MMB, you may also rapidly change the range in both the horizontal and vertical directions.

❖ **Workspaces**

Blender 4.3 workspaces are customized settings made to maximize your productivity for particular jobs. The way that editors and panels are arranged in each workspace takes into account the many facets of the 3D development process. An overview of the default workspaces and instructions for managing and modifying them to suit your requirements can be found here.

- **Default Workspace**

1. Layout
   - General-purpose workspace for basic operations, scene setup, and 3D modeling.
   - Editors: Timeline, Properties, Outliner, and 3D Viewport.
   - Use: Perfect for basic modeling, object handling, and scene setup.
2. Modeling:
   - Purpose: Focused on detailed 3D modeling tasks.
   - Editors: 3D Viewport with a tool shelf, Outliner, Properties, and a smaller Timeline.
   - Usage: Optimized for creating and editing mesh objects with modeling tools.
3. Sculpting:
   - Purpose: Dedicated to digital sculpting and high-detail modeling.
   - Editors: 3D Viewport with sculpting tools, Tool Settings, and a smaller Outliner.
   - Usage: Provides access to various brushes and sculpting options for high-resolution detail work.
4. UV Editing:
   - Purpose: Specialized for UV mapping and texture editing.
   - Editors: 3D Viewport and UV/Image Editor side by side.
   - Usage: Facilitates unwrapping 3D models and editing UV maps for texturing.
5. Texture Paint:

- Purpose: Designed for painting textures directly onto 3D models.
- Editors: 3D Viewport, UV/Image Editor, and Tool Settings.
- Usage: Access to painting tools and options for creating detailed textures.

6. Shading:
   - Purpose: Focused on creating and editing materials and shaders.
   - Editors: 3D Viewport, Shader Editor, and a smaller Outliner.
   - Usage: Node-based workflow for creating complex materials.

7. Animation:
   - Purpose: Optimized for creating and editing animations.
   - Editors: 3D Viewport, Timeline, Dope Sheet, and Graph Editor.
   - Usage: Keyframe animation, managing animation curves, and fine-tuning motion.

8. Rendering:
   - Purpose: Focused on rendering scenes and adjusting render settings.
   - Editors: 3D Viewport, Properties, and Image Editor.
   - Usage: Preview renders, adjust render settings, and manage render outputs.

9. Compositing:
   - Purpose: For post-processing and compositing rendered images and animations.
   - Editors: Node Editor, Image Editor, and a smaller 3D Viewport.

- Usage: Node-based compositing for adding effects and combining images.

10. Scripting:
    - Purpose: Dedicated to scripting and automation using Python.
    - Editors: Text Editor, 3D Viewport, and Console.
    - Usage: Write and test Python scripts to extend Blender's functionality.

- **Managing and Customizing Workspaces**

Creating a New Workspace:

- Add Workspace: Click the "+" button next to the existing workspaces.
- Choose Template: Select a template or start from an existing workspace.
- Customize Layout: Arrange editors and panels to fit your workflow.
- Save Workspace: Name your workspace and save it for future use.

Modifying an Existing Workspace:

- Drag and Drop Editors: Rearrange editors by dragging their headers.
- Split/Join Areas: Right-click the border between editors to split or join areas.
- Adjust Editor Types: Change the type of editor by clicking the editor's header and selecting a new type.
- Save Changes: Blender automatically saves your workspace layout, but you can also save it as part of your startup file (File > Defaults > Save Startup File).

Switching Workspaces:

- Workspace Tabs: Click on the workspace tabs at the top of the Blender window.
- Shortcut Keys: Use shortcut keys (Ctrl + Page Up/Page Down) to switch between workspaces quickly.

Deleting a Workspace:

- Right-Click Tab: Right-click on the workspace tab you want to delete.
- Delete Workspace: Select "Delete Workspace" from the context menu.

❖ **Status Bar**

Blender 4.3's Status Bar may be found at the bottom of the Blender window. It helps you keep informed about the progress of your project and streamlines some processes by offering rapid access to a variety of features and useful information. Below is a comprehensive rundown of the elements and functionalities of the Status Bar:

▪ **Component of the Status Bar**

1. Active Tool and Tool Settings
   - Description: Shows the active tool along with its main settings.
   - Use: Access key settings and quickly check which tool is active without leaving the 3D Viewport or other editors.
2. Selection Info:

- Description: Shows information about the current selection, such as the number of selected vertices, edges, faces, or objects.
- Usage: Helpful for keeping track of what you have selected, especially in complex scenes or while editing meshes.

3. Scene Statistics:
    - Description: Provides an overview of the scene, including the total number of objects, vertices, edges, faces, and other elements.
    - Usage: Useful for monitoring the complexity of your scene and ensuring optimal performance.

4. Active Object Information:
    - Description: Displays the name and type of the currently active object.
    - Usage: Helps you quickly identify the active object and switch context if needed.

5. Playback Controls:
    - Description: Controls for playing, pausing, and navigating through the timeline.
    - Usage: Essential for animation work, allowing you to preview and scrub through your animations directly from the Status Bar.

6. Message Area:
    - Description: Displays contextual messages, warnings, and error notifications.
    - Usage: Keeps you informed about important events, such as successful operations, errors, or warnings that require your attention.

7. Context-Sensitive Options:

- Description: Provides additional options and information based on the current context and active tools.
- Usage: Enhances workflow efficiency by offering quick access to relevant functions and settings.

❖ **Tabs and Panels**

▪ **Tabs**

The user interface's overlapping portions are managed with tabs. Only one Tab's content is displayed at once. A tab header, which can be vertical or horizontal, contains a list of tabs.

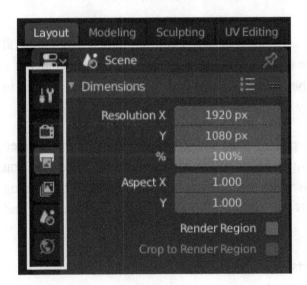

Switching or Cycling

Ctrl+Wheel may be used to flip between vertical tabs from anyplace in the tab. Additionally, you may use Shift+Ctrl+Tab and Ctrl+Tab to cycle across tabs, or you can use LMB to depress the mouse and drag it over each of the tab heading icons.

- ▪ **Panels**

A panel is the smallest structural element in the user interface. The panel's title is displayed in the panel header. It is constantly apparent. Subpanels are also included in certain panels.

- • **Position**

A panel's location inside its area may be adjusted by clicking on and dragging on the grip widget (::::) located on the header's right side.

- • **Pinning**

It can be useful to simultaneously examine panels from several tabs at times. For example, being able to view the attributes of a camera while other items are selected. The solution to this is to enable pinnability for panels.

Whichever tab is picked does not affect the visibility of a pinned panel. By selecting the pin icon located in the panel's header, you may pin it. Panels without a pin symbol can be pinned by holding down Shift-LMB or right-clicking on the panel header and choosing Pin.

- ▪ **Presets**

- • **Selector**

A selection of the available settings. The bundled properties will be superseded by a selection.

- • **Add +**

Based on the set of attributes that are now applied, new presets can be added and saved for later use. When a pop-up window appears, you may choose a name from the list and, in some situations, modify other parameters.

- **Remove –**

Removes the chosen setting.

❖ **Shortcuts**

  ▪ **Keyboard Shortcuts**

This handbook displays hotkey letters as they would look on a keyboard, such as:

- **G**is referring to the lowercase g.
- **Ctrl, Shift, Alt**
  Are specified as modifier keys.
- **Ctrl+W, Shift+Alt+A**
  Suggests that pressing these keys at the same time is recommended.
- **Numpad0-Numpad9, NumpadPlus**
  Refer to the keys that is on the separate numeric keypad.
- Some other keys are referred to by their names, such as **Esc, Tab, F1 to F12**. Of special note are the arrow keys, **Left, Right** and others.

  ▪ **Mouse**

Mouse buttons are referred to in this document as:

- **LMB**

  Left Mouse Button

- **RMB**
  Right Mouse Button
- **MMB**
  Middle Mouse Button
- **Wheel, WheelUp & WheelDown**
  Scrolling the wheel.

  - **Hovering**

While the pointer is lingering (over a button).

Properties

- Ctrl + C: Copy the selected value of the button.

- Ctrl + V: Paste the selected value of the button.

- Ctrl + Alt + C: Copy the whole color of vector of the field.

- Ctrl + Alt + V: Paste the whole color of the field.

- RMB: Open the menu of the context.

- Backspace: Delete the value.

- Minus: Translate number values (multiply by -1.0).

- Ctrl + Wheel: Change the incremental value steps.

  For pop-up option menus buttons, this cycles the value.

- Return: Turn on menus or toggles the value.

- Alt: In order to make changes to all of the chosen items, hold down when altering values. (objects, bones, sequence-strips).

Number fields and toggles these shortcuts can be use.

- **Animation**

- I: Input a keyframe.

- Alt + I: Delete the keyframe.

- Shift + Alt + I: Delete all keyframes.

- Ctrl + D: Assigning a driver.

- Ctrl + Alt + D: Delete the driver.

- K: Inserting a Keying Set.

- Alt + K: Deleting the Keying Set.

- **Python Scripting**

- Ctrl + C: When you hover over any Operational Buttons, the corresponding Python command is copied to the clipboard. You may use this in the Text editor or Python Console to write scripts.
- Shift + Ctrl + C: Their data path for this property is copied by hovering over property buttons.
- Shift + Ctrl + Alt + C: Overproperty buttons replicate the data-block and property's entire data flow. Keep in mind

that it is usually preferable to retrieve items by context rather than by name.

- **Dragging**

- Ctrl: Snap to discrete steps, when dragging.

- Shift: This gives control over values in the field.

- Shift + Ctrl: The item will be precisely moved by precise snap in addition to the snapping limitation.

- **Text Editing**

- Home: Move to the beginning of the line.

- End: Move to the ending part of the line.

- Left, Right: Take the cursor for a single move.

- Ctrl + Left, Ctrl + Right: Take the cursor for an entire word.

- Backspace, Delete: Remove characters.

- Ctrl + Backspace, Ctrl + Delete: Remove words.

- Shift: Choose while pressing down the key and moving the cursor.

- Ctrl + A: Choose all text.

- Ctrl + C: Copy the highlighted text.

- Ctrl + X: Cut the highlighted text.

- Ctrl + V – Paste text at the position of the cursor.

❖ Buttons

Operator Buttons

When an operator button is pressed with LMB, an operator is executed, which, in essence, performs an operation. Operator buttons can be text, an icon, or an icon combined with text.

Toggle Buttons and Checkbox

Options can be activated or deactivated using these controls. To alter their status, use LMB. Checkboxes with a tick indicate that the option is active. Toggle buttons' active status is shown by a change in icon images or a change in color on the icon backdrop.

Dragging

You may drag over numerous buttons while holding down the LMB button to turn multiple settings at once on or off. This may be used to choose a radio button value, toggle buttons, and checkboxes.

❖ Fields

▪ Search and Text Field

Text fields have a rectangular border that is rounded, and they may also have an icon or text inside of them. Text fields are used to store text strings and offer conventional text editing shortcuts for text editing.

▪ Number Field

Units and values are stored in number fields.

When the mouse pointer is above the first kind of number field, angles indicating left (<) and right (>) are displayed on the field's sides.

A second kind of number field is called a slider, which shows numbers throughout a range, such as percentage values, with a colored bar in the backdrop.

- **Multi-value Editing**

By holding down **LMB** on the first field and dragging vertically over the fields you wish to modify, you may edit several number fields at once. Lastly, you have two options: release the LMB and put in a valueor use the mouse to drag left or right to alter the value.

- **Value Limit**

"Soft limit" and "hard limit" value ranges limit the majority of numerical values. Only the "soft limit" value range may be changed by dragging with the mouse. Wider value ranges can be used when entering data via a keyboard, but they can never go above the "hard limit."

- **Color Field**

A color value is kept in the color field. Using LMB to click on it brings up the Color Picker.

Alpha channel color fields are split in half: the color is displayed without an alpha channel on the left, and with an alpha channel over a checkerboard pattern on the right. You may drag and drop colors to other color areas to copy them.

When you hover your cursor over a color attribute, a huge preview of the color and its RGBA, HSVA, and hexadecimal values will appear.

❖ **Decorators**

Small buttons called decorators that display the property's condition are positioned to the right of other buttons. Checkboxes, menus, and number fields may all have decorators next to them to show that the feature is animated.

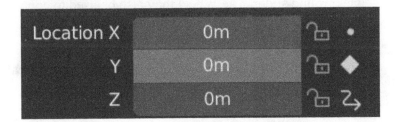

When the decoration dot icon is clicked, a Key-frame is added to that property. To eliminate the key-frame, simply click the rhombus icon once again. When a rhombus icon is solid, it means that a key-frame is present on the current frame; when it is not solid, it means that the attribute has a key-frame on a different frame. A key-frame with the currently selected value will be created on the current frame when you click the non-solid rhombus symbol.

The decorator displays the driver icon when one property is being driven by another.

Decorators streamline the process of quickly assessing a property's condition.

❖ Color Picker

You may provide a color value using the color picker, a pop-up window. To quickly choose primary colors, hold down the Ctrl key while dragging.

- Palette
  Allows you to select the primary and secondary color elements. You can alter the shape; see to Types.
- Slider for Colors
  The third color part may be defined using the gradient-background slider. The Wheel may also be used to control it.
- Model Color
  Choose the Color Model for the following numerical fields.
  HSV/HSL, Hex, and RGB

❖ Curve Widget

Using a curve with the X and Y axes representing the input and output, the Curve Widget makes it simple to transfer an assortment of value inputs to a set of output values.

Control points

Control points are used to manipulate the Curve Widget's curve, much like they do with any other Blender curve.

In other words, the input is mapped exactly to the output (unchanged) at (0.0, 0.0) and (1.0, 1.0), where there are two control points by default.

❖ **Node**

In Blender, every node has a similar foundation. This is true for all kinds of nodes. These components include of the attributes, sockets, title, and more.

Inputs

The node's inputs, which are on its bottom left, supply the information required for the node to function. When unplugged, each input socket—aside from the green shader input—has a default value that may be changed via a color, numeric, or vector interface input. A color interface input determines the second color choice in the node screenshot above.

Certain nodes are equipped with unique sockets that support several inputs. Instead of a circle, these sockets will have an ellipsis to represent their unique behavior.

Output

The node's upper right section has its outputs, which can be linked to nodes lower in the node tree via their inputs.

- **Frame Node**

By assembling similar nodes in one location, the Frame node helps organize nodes. When a node arrangement grows complicated and extensive, frames come in handy, although they are not necessary if a node group may be reused.

- Label Dimensions

Label font size. For instance, smaller titles for subordinate frames.

- Diminish

The frame shrinks around a node after it is inserted to eliminate unnecessary space. Resizing of the Frame now happens automatically as nodes inside it are rearranged; it is no longer necessary to pick the edge of the Frame to resize it. Disabling this option will alter this behavior.

- Text

Frame nodes can show a text data-block's contents when you need to present text that is more thorough. You will have to edit the contents using the Text Editor because this is read-only.

- **Reroute Node**

A node is a structure that is mostly utilized for organizing. In that it allows numerous output connections while supporting just one input connection, reroute functions and looks a lot like a socket on other nodes.

Holding Shift and RMB while sweeping across the link will add a Reroute node to an existing connection rapidly.

❖ **Operators**

Activating an operator initiates an action; this distinguishes operators from tools, which need input. Popup menus, menu searches, or operator buttons can all be used to initiate an operator. Operators can be used to add, remove, or change an object's shading from sharp to smooth.

Operator Properties

The majority of operators have attributes that can be changed to improve the outcome. Modify the attributes in the Adjust Last Action section after running the operator (which will utilize its default settings).

Modal Operators

Between normal operators and tools, there is a notion known as modal operators. They need interactive input of some kind.

With LMB or Return, a modal operator's activity may be verified. Use Esc or RMB to cancel a modal operator.

Slider Operators

In the editor's Header, a percentage number may be interactively changed using slider operators.

Drag the slider to the left or right to change the percentage. Holding Ctrl will make this coarser (snapping in 10% increments), and holding Shift will make it more precise. You can use the letter E to toggle "overshoot" on several sliders, allowing you to move outside of the 0–100% range.

CHAPTER 4: Modelling

A 3D scene requires three fundamental elements: models, materials, and lighting. The first of these, modeling, is covered in this section. To put it simply, modeling is the art and science of creating a surface that either represents your abstract image of goods or replicates the shape of an actual object.

Modes

When modeling, switching between modes is typical. While certain tools might only be available in one mode, others might only be available in many modes.

Modes Editing

The primary mode used for modeling is called Edit Mode. To alter the following kinds of items, utilize alter Mode:

- Meshes
- Bends
- Surfaces
- Metaballs
- Textual elements
- Lattice

Only the items' mesh may be altered when altering them. You can utilize Multi-Object Editing, exit Edit Mode, and pick another object to alter it, among other options.

❖ **Mesh**

Mesh modeling often begins with mesh primitive forms like cubes, cylinders, and circles. After that, you might begin modifying to create a larger, more complex shape.

- **Structure**

Everything in a mesh is constructed from three fundamental components: faces, edges, and vertices.

Vertices

A vertex (plural of vertices) is a single point or place in three dimensions that is the most basic part of a mesh. In edit mode, vertices in the 3D Viewport are shown by little dots. The vertices of an object are stored in an array of coordinates.

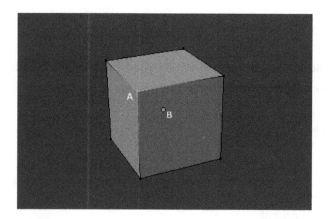

Edge

A straight line connecting two vertices is usually called an edge. The edges are the "wires" that are visible when viewing a mesh in wireframe mode. They are typically not visible in the final image. They are used to make faces.

Faces

The actual surface of the item is created using faces. These are what you see when the model is rendered. If there are no faces in this area of the projected image, it will be transparent or nonexistent.

The area between three (triangles), four (quadrangles), or more (n-gons) vertices that has edges on all sides is called a face. The faces are commonly shortened to tris, quads, and n-gons. Because triangles are always flat, they are easy to calculate. In contrast, quadrangles "deform well," which makes them the preferred shape for animation and subdivision modeling.

Shading

The way light interacts with three-dimensional objects is greatly influenced by surface normals, which in turn impacts how those objects are shaded. The shading of normals might be smooth or flat.

Using flat shading creates and displays the faces of a mesh uniformly. This is frequently used for objects with flat surfaces, such as cubes and pyramids.

By enabling seamless transitions between adjacent polygons—which are accomplished by interpolating the normals across a polygonal mesh's vertices—smooth shading offers a mesh a more realistic appearance.

By default, face normals have flat shading, but you may alter this for individual faces or the entire object.

- **Topology**

Loop

Edge and face loops, as seen in Fig., are groups of faces or edges that form ongoing "loops." loops on the face and edges.

The loops (1 and 3) in the previous image that do not end in a pole are cyclic. Beginning and finishing at the same vertex, they divided the model in half. In organic character animation, loops are essential for handling distinct, continuous portions of a mesh in a fast and efficient manner.

Edge Loop

The loops of edges in Fig. Loops 1 and 2 are edge and face loops. They connect vertices in such a way that each vertex on the loop has exactly two neighbors who are not on the loop and are positioned on both sides of the loop, except for the start and end vertices in the case of poles.

The concept of edge loops is essential, especially in organic (subsurface) modeling and character animation. When used properly, they enable you to produce models with a small number of vertices that appear highly realistic when used as subdivision surfaces and deform nicely in animation.

Examine Fig. Face edges and loops. In biological modeling, for example, the edge loops follow the natural lines of deformation and forms of the underlying muscles and skin. The loops are thicker in areas like the shoulders and knees where the figure moves more than in other areas.

- **Mirrors**

Mirror allows you to change vertices along the chosen axis symmetrically. Through symmetry along the chosen axis, an element (vertex, edge, or face) will be transformed in accordance with its identical axis-mirrored counterpart (in local space), if one exists.

Mirror of Topology

When working on a mirrored Mesh Geometry using any of the three Mirror Axis options, the mirrored vertices need to be positioned exactly. Vertices that are not exactly in their mirror orientations will not be treated as reflected by the Mirror Axis.

Magnitude order In order to find mirrored vertices, Mirror looks at both their positions and their connections to other vertices in the Mesh Geometry. It takes into account the entire topology when determining which vertices will be regarded as mirrors. As a result, mirrored vertices that are not symmetrical can nevertheless be regarded as mirrored.

Auto Merge

Magnitude order In order to find mirrored vertices, Mirror looks at both their positions and their connections to other vertices in the Mesh Geometry. It takes into account the entire topology when determining which vertices will be regarded as mirrors. As a result, mirrored vertices that are not symmetrical can nevertheless be regarded as mirrored.

▪ Primitives

One common object type in 3D scenes is a mesh. Blender comes with a lot of "primitive" mesh shapes so you can start sculpting straight away. Additionally, the 3D cursor in Edit Mode may be used to add primitives.

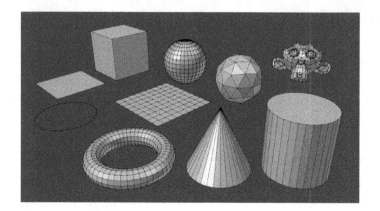

Common Options

The Adjust Last Operation panel displays when the item is created and allows you to choose these choices. Among the options found in many primitives are:

Produce UVs

Creates a new geometry's default UV unwrapping. The initial UV layer (which may be added as needed) will define this.

Size and Radius, Orient to View, Place, and Rotate

Cube

A typical cube is a three-dimensional shape with eight vertices, twelve edges, and six faces. Dice, boxes, and crates are among the items that may be made out of cubes.

Plane

Meshes are a popular kind of object in 3D sceneries. Many "primitive" mesh shapes are included with Blender so you may begin sculpting right away. Primitives can also be added using the 3D cursor in Edit Mode.

UV Sphere

Quad faces plus a triangular fan at the top and bottom make up a typical UV sphere. Texturing can be done using it.

Icosphere

A polyhedral sphere composed of triangles is called an icosphere. Icospheres are typically employed to create a vertices arrangement that is more isotropical—that is, uniform in all directions—than a UV sphere.

- **Extrude Region**

Extrusion tools are used to duplicate vertices, however the geometry that is produced is still connected to the original vertices. Vertices develop into edges, which in turn develop into faces.

This tool is essential for creating new geometry. It makes it easy to construct things like tree branches and to create cylinders from circles and parallelepipeds from rectangles.

The axis along which vertices and edges are extruded can be interactively set. Faces are extruded along their mean normal by default. Extrusion can be limited to one axis by defining one axis (see Axis Locking).

The extrude tools differ in how they join the new geometry.

Details

Even though Extrude is a fairly simple method, the following talk explores the highly sophisticated concepts that underpin it:

- First, the algorithm determines which of the selected edges will become the extrude's outer edge loop, or face. • Faces are then generated from the edges in the edge loop. By default, the algorithm considers edges that belong to two or more selected faces to be internal (see below), which means they are not included in the loop.

- If the edges in the edge loop match only one face in the whole mesh, then all of the selected faces are duplicated and linked to the newly created faces. Rectangles, for example, will result in parallelepipeds at this level.

- In other cases, the selected faces are linked to the newly created faces rather than being replicated. Unwanted faces are therefore prevented from remaining "inside" the finished mesh. This difference is important because it ensures that consistently coherent, closed volumes are created whenever Extrude is employed.

- Because the volume is duplicated independently of the original, extrusion only creates a duplication for fully closed volumes (such a cube with all six faces).

- Edges that are not a part of the chosen faces create a "open" edge loop. These edges are copied, and the new edge is joined to the old edge to create a new face.

- A new edge is formed between two single selected vertices that do not belong to any selected edges by duplicating them.

❖ Curves

Surfaces and curves are two examples of Blender object types. They are expressed as mathematical functions (interpolation) rather than as linear interpolation between a group of locations. Blender offers Bézier curves and NURBS. An arrangement of "control points" (sometimes called "control vertices") forms the "control polygon" and produces Bézier curves as well as NURBS curves and surfaces.

NURBS and Bézier curves are named after their mathematical definitions, although choosing one over the other often depends more on how each is internally computed than on how a modeler would see them. Bezier curves are frequently simpler to comprehend since they start and end at the control points you choose; nevertheless, NURBS curves are simpler for computers to calculate when a curve contains several twists and turns.

The primary benefit of utilizing curves in modeling instead of polygonal meshes is that, because they require less data to describe, curves can provide outcomes with lower memory and storage requirements. However, greater render times might result from this procedural surface management.

For certain modeling processes, such extruding a profile along a path, curves are the only tool available. Vertex-level control is more difficult with curve modeling, though. Mesh editing could be a better modeling option if exact control is needed. Bezier curves are the most often used curves for designing lettering and logos.

- **Tools**

Type

The kind of curve to draw using.

- Poly:

Straight line segments in a Bézier curve (auto handles).

- Bézier: Tolerance

Higher numbers provide more smoothed results, while lower values produce a result that is more similar to the drawing stroke.

Technique

- Redesign:

Refit the curve incrementally to get the best results.

- Divided:

Creates a better drawing performance by splitting the curve till the tolerance is reached.

Detect Corners

uses a specified angle as the foundation for detecting corners in drawings; any angle larger than the specified value is considered a corner. The curve uses non-aligned handles to identify a corner, resulting in a more accurate corner.

- **Transform Panels**

When nothing is selected, the panel is blank. When many vertices are selected, the median values are modified and "Median" is added before the labels.

Control point, Vertex

The coordinates of the chosen point or handle (vertex) are displayed by the initial controls (X, Y, Z). When dealing with a NURBS curve, the weight of the chosen control point, or the median weight, is defined by the fourth component that is accessible (W).

Radius

Regulates the bevel or extrusion width along the "spinal" curve. From one point to another, the radius will be interpolated (you can check it using the normals).

Tilt

Governs how each control point's normals, which are represented as arrows, twist; hence, it only matters for 3D curves! From one point to the next, the tilt will be interpolated (you can check it using the normals).

Space

You may select whether those coordinates are relative to the global origin (global) or the object origin (local) using the Space radio buttons.

Local Global

Weight

Regulates the "goal weight" of a subset of control points. This is utilized in the case of Soft Body physics curves, which force the curve to "stick" to its initial locations in relation to the weight.

❖ Surface

Surfaces are the 3D extension of curves, which are 2D objects. But take note that Blender only allows you to work with NURBS surfaces—no Bézier (though you may use the Bézier knot type; see below) or polygonal surfaces—you can use meshes for these instead. Curves and surfaces are not the same thing, even though they belong to the same object type (as do texts). For instance, you cannot have both curves and surfaces in the same object.

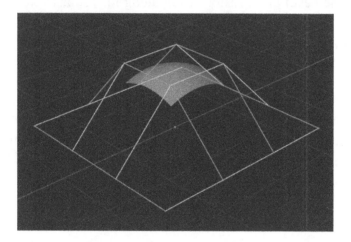

Since surfaces are 2D, they have two interpolation axes: U (like curves) and V. It is important to understand that you have independent control over the interpolation rules (knot, order, and resolution) for each of these two dimensions (the U and V fields for all these parameters, of course).

One could ask, "But the surface seems to be 3D, why is it only 2D?" For an object to be deemed three-dimensional, it must possess "Volume"; a surface, even when closed, is devoid of volume due to its infinite thinness. If the surface had a volume, it may also have a thickness, which is its third dimension. As a result, it can only be regarded as a 2D object with a maximum of two interpolation dimensions, axes, or coordinates (surfaces are really non-Euclidean 2D planes, if you know what I mean). Rolling a piece of paper into a cylinder is a more "real-world" example. The sheet will become a "volume" yet remain a (almost) 2D entity!

Conversion

There is no "internal" conversion in this case because there are simply NURBS surfaces.

There is, however, a surface to mesh "external" conversion that is limited to using in Object Mode. It converts a surface object into a mesh object by creating faces, edges, and vertices using the surface resolutions in both directions.

Visualization

NURBS surfaces in Edit Mode, there is almost no difference from NURBS curves other than the fact that the U direction is represented by yellow grid lines and the V direction is realized by pink grid lines.

Similar to curves, control points can be hidden or made visible.

- **Rows and Grid, Control Points**

NURBS curves and surfaces have the same control points. However, their design is quite limiting. The concept of a "segment" is eliminated, and "rows" and the "grid" as a whole take their   place.
A row is a group of control points that form a single "line" in a single interpolation direction, much to edge loops for meshes. As a result, a NURBS surface has "U rows" and "V rows." It's crucial to keep in mind that each row of a certain kind (U or V) has an equal number of control points. Each control point has exactly one U row and one V row.

All of this results in a "grid," or "cage," whose shape dictates the shape of the NURBS surface. Sort of like a lattice It is important to realize that a NURBS surface cannot have an individual control point added to it. With exactly the same number of control points as the other rows, you must instead create a whole U or V row all at once (in practice, you would probably add them using the Extrude tool or perhaps the Duplicate one). Moreover, it suggests that you can only "merge" different surface pieces if at least one of their rows correspond.

Weight

Similar to NURBS Splines, NURBS Surface control points offer a weight feature. The weight characteristic of the control point determines its effect on the surface. This weight should not be confused with the Goal Weight, which is only used for soft body simulations. The NURBS control point weight may be adjusted in the W number field on the Transform panel.

Fig. displays a single control point with a weight of 5. One control point, "C," has its weight set to 5.0, while all other control points have their weights set to 1.0 by default. The surface is clearly being pulled in the direction of that control point.

Preset Weights

NURBS may be used to produce pure shapes, such as circles, cylinders, and spheres (a Bézier circle is not a pure circle). To create pure circles, spheres, or cylinders, you must set the control point weights to the appropriate values. Since this is not immediately apparent, you should educate yourself about NURBS before proceeding.

The concept for making a 2D circle is the same as that for making a sphere out of 2D surfaces. It is clear that a sphere requires four different weights: 1.0, 0.707 = sqrt(0.5), 0.354 = sqrt(2)/4, and 0.25.

- **Shapes**

Preview Resolution U/V

Optimal resolution for the 3D Viewport.

Produce U/V

Similar to NURBS curves, resolution controls the amount of detail on the surface. The higher the resolution, the smoother and more detailed the surface. The Resolution decreases with surface roughness. In this instance, however, you have two resolution settings: one for the interpolation axis U and V.

You may individually adjust the resolution for the preview and render to prevent viewport latency and preserve high-quality renderings.

❖ Metaball

Similar to NURBS curves, resolution controls the amount of detail on the surface. The higher the resolution, the smoother and more detailed the surface. The Resolution decreases with surface roughness. In this instance, however, you have two resolution settings: one for the interpolation axis U and V. You may individually adjust the resolution for the preview and render to prevent viewport latency and preserve high-quality renderings.

You may use the Active Element panel to switch between any of them at any moment. any of these is determined by its own underlying mathematical structure.

Meta objects are typically used as a foundation for modeling or for special effects. For instance, you may start your model's shape with a group of metas and turn it into a mesh for additional modeling or sculpting. Ray tracing can also benefit greatly from the use of meta objects.

Visualization

The computed mesh and a black "selection ring" are displayed in Object Mode.

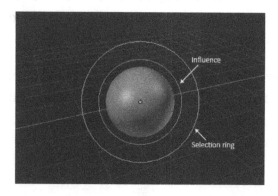

In Edit Mode, a meta is shown as a mesh (either tinted or as a black wireframe, but obviously without any vertices) (Fig. Meta Ball in Edit Mode). It has two colored circles: a green circle for direct control of the stiffness of the meta (light green when active) and a red circle for selection (pink when chosen). Remember that, except from the scale shift, having the green circle highlighted is equivalent to having the red one.

❖ **Text**

Text objects belong to the same object type family as curves and surfaces because fonts are vector data, which is made up of curves. In Blender, letter codes are mapped to the corresponding geometry in the 3D Viewport using a "Font System." In addition to its own built-in typeface, this font system supports external fonts including PostScript Type 1, OpenType, and TrueType. Additionally, it may use any object in the current blend-file to make letters.

Text objects allow you to create and display 2D or 3D text with a wide range of complex layout options, including justifying and frames. Letters are essentially just flat filled surfaces by default, just like any closed 2D curve. But, much as with curves, you may extrude them and apply modifiers to them (e.g. to make them follow a curve). Text may be arranged in Blender in a variety of quite complex ways, including by using different alignments, constructing columns or text blocks, and more.

- **Text Editing**

Text editing in Blender is largely done in two locations and differs greatly from editing other kinds of objects. The first place you enter text is in the 3D Viewport. There are certain shortcuts for applying styles, for instance (see Font); but, the majority of Blender shortcuts that you are accustomed to using in Edit Mode do not work with text. Second are the Properties, especially the Font tab.

- **Copy**

Use the shortcut or the corresponding Edit menu option to copy text to the buffer (Ctrl + C).

- **Cut**

Use the shortcut or the appropriate Edit menu option to cut and copy text to the buffer (Ctrl + x).

- **Paste**

Use the shortcut or the corresponding Edit menu option to paste text from the buffer (Ctrl + v).

- **To Upper Case**

Converts the chosen text's case to uppercase (Header ‣ Text ‣ Upper Case).

- **To Lower Case**

Converts the chosen text's case to lowercase (Header ‣ Text ‣ Lower Case).

- **To Paste File**

Text from an external text file is inserted. This will open a File Browser so you may open a legitimate UTF-8 file. As always, take care that there aren't too many characters in the file because this can slow down interactive response (Header ‣ Text ‣ Paste File).

- **Insert Unicode**

Enables the input of any Unicode character by its hexadecimal codepoint value in a dialog box (Header ‣Text ‣ Insert Unicode).

- **Applying Bold, Underline**

You may either choose the text that already exists and then toggle the chosen style from the menu, or you can switch on the corresponding setting before inputting any letters to apply the Bold, Italics, Underline, or Small Caps attribute to that set of characters.

- **Special Characters**

This character map is restricted to inserting characters that aren't accessible using the keyboard. You can "compose" a lot of different special characters; see Accent Characters. You'll have to copy and paste them from an external editor or character map software if you need more (Header ›Text › Special Character).

❖ **Volume**

OpenVDB files are represented in Blender as containers called volume objects. OpenVDB is a file format and library for volumetric data transfer and storage. Programs such as Houdini or Blender's fluid simulation cache may generate OpenVDB files. Using the Add menu in the 3D Viewport or by dragging and dropping vdb-files into Blender, you may create volume objects. Animations may be created by loading the frame sequence from an OpenVDB file.

Rendering Volume

Volumes and simulations of rendering smoke work similarly. The Principled Volume shader is used by default for rendering volume objects. It will utilize the temperature, color, and density grids by default. If the shader nodes are inaccessible, a replacement grid name must be used.

Limitations

OpenVDB provides a good representation of sparse volumes, which can be scattered over space instead of being confined to a tiny bounding box. In Blender, these are still rendered as thick volumes, which is not optimal for performance or memory use.

This will be improved in later iterations. OpenVDB files may also be used to store level sets and points. Although level set grids may be read, they are currently not supported when shown as surfaces. There is no support for OpenVDB point imports.

❖ **Empties**

With no extra geometry, the "empty" is only a single coordinate point that may be used for a variety of applications as a handle. However, because it lacks a surface and volume, it cannot be displayed.

▪ **Primitives**

● **Plain Axes**

Originally appears as six lines, one for the +X, -X, +Y, -Y, +Z, and -Z axis directions.

● **Arrows**

Appears as labeled arrows that are originally oriented in the positive X, Y, and Z axis orientations.

● **Single Arrow**

Appears as a single arrow that points in the direction of the +Z axis at first.

● **Image**

Images can be shown in empty spaces. Using this, reference pictures such as character sheets or blueprints may be produced for modeling purposes. Regardless of the 3D display setting, the picture is presented.

You can go to the Empty Displays settings from Properties ›
Object Data › Empty panel.

CHAPTER 5: UV Editors

UV maps, which specify how a 2D picture should be mapped onto a 3D object, are edited using the UV Editor.

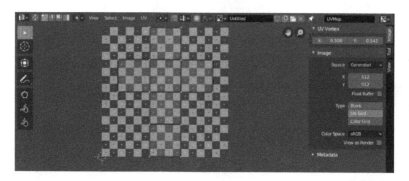

Image textures are typically used when procedural textures are not homogenous or creating the desired appearance is challenging. For example, a car's body would not be covered with random scratches; instead, they would occur in strategic spots. Many projections (Box, Sphere, etc.) in Blender may be used to automatically apply a 2D image to a 3D object, however they are often confined to simple meshes. For more complicated ones, a UV map must be created. This is a flat zone where the 2D picture's faces of 3D objects are placed, indicating which section of the image should be utilized as texture. You now have complete control over the mapping technique.

The axes of the map—V for vertical and U for horizontal—are symbolized by the word "UV." These symbols were employed to avoid confusion with the letters "X" and "Y," which represent 3D axes.

The easiest way to teach UV mapping is to pull open a cardboard box. It could be spread out flat on a tabletop if you slashed along its edges with scissors. When looking down at the table, we may argue that U represents the left-right orientation and V represents the up-down direction.

The next step may be to place the unfolded box on top of a poster, cut the poster to suit the measurements of the box, glue the poster to the box, and then reassemble the box. You now have a 2D image that is textured on a 3D box.

A UV map depicts the box's placement on the poster as well as the cutting pattern. You have complete control over how this is done; if you wish, you may cut each side of the box separately and position, scale, rotate, and even skew it on the poster independently of the other sides.

Example

The picture above depicts a three-dimensional dome flattening into a disk in ultraviolet space. Next, each 3D face is textured with the UV map region of the image it covers.

The image also contains distortion, which is a common issue with UV mapping. Observe how the checkered squares in the 2D texture are all the same size, but when applied to the 3D dome, they change size—they are smaller at the top than at the base. This is due to the flattening process, which causes the faces in the UV map to differ in relative size from those in 3D space.

Usually, you'll want to reduce this distortion by hand-guiding and fine-tuning the flattening—you might use seams, for instance. It isn't always feasible to get rid of it entirely, though.

❖ 2D Cursor

Similar to the 3D Viewport, the UV Editor has a Cursor that may be accessed by selecting View ▸ Center View to Cursor. It can also function as a snapping target and pivot point.

To move the Cursor, use Shift + RMB with any tool, or LMB with the Cursor tool selected. You may also alter the "Location X/Y" fields in the Sidebar's View tab using pixel values or relative coordinates (0 to 1). In all instances, the origin (0, 0) is in the picture's lower left corner.

To bring the cursor to the middle, press Shift + C.

❖ Overlays

There is a button in the header that disables the UV Editor's overlays completely. In addition, this option controls whether UDIM tile information is displayed. The drop-down menu prompts a pop-up with more detailed settings. The following categories are available:

- Grid
  Display the grid.
- Above Image
  Instead of behind the image, display the grid on top of it.
- Source of Grid Shape

How counts are calculated for rows and columns.

❖ **Selecting**

The UV Editor features a Select menu and buttons for selecting modes in the header, just like the 3D Viewport.

▪ **Sync Selection**

When the UV Editor is switched off, it only displays the faces that are selected in the 3D Viewport by default. When an object is selected in one editor, it may not be picked in the other. If a single 3D vertex or edge corresponds to many UV vertices or edges, you can choose them individually.

When the UV Editor is turned on, it always displays all of the faces. When you choose an item in one editor, it is also chosen in the other. You may only choose the UV vertices and edges that correspond to a single 3D vertex or edge; you cannot select individual vertices or edges.

▪ **Mode of Selection**

Vertex: 1 Pick out the vertices.

Edge: Two chosen edges.

Face: Three chosen faces.

Island: 4 Choose adjacent face groupings. Available only when Sync Selection is turned off.

If Sync Selection is enabled, you may expand/contract the selection by pressing Ctrl, or you can hold Shift while selecting a selection mode to activate multiple ones at once.

- **Sticky Selection mode**

Options to choose extra UV vertices automatically. Available only when Sync Selection is turned off.

- Disable

It is possible to choose each UV vertex separately from the others.

- Shared Location

UV vertices with the same UV coordinates and matching mesh vertex will be automatically selected. This is the default and creates the appearance that numerous faces in a UV map can share a vertex, whereas in fact they each have an overlap of distinct vertices.

- Mutual Vertex

Choose UV vertices that are automatically assigned to the same mesh vertex, regardless of the differences in their UV coordinates. When you activate Sync Selection, the behavior remains the same.

- ❖ **Snapping**

UV elements may be readily aligned with other components by snapping. Toggle it on and off using the magnet icon in the UV Editor's header or, for a shorter time, hold down the Ctrl key. This page discusses the Snap header button; for the Snap menu, go to UV Editing.

- **Snap Target**

- Increase

Snaps into place at grid locations.

This option allows you to snap to an artificial grid with the same resolution as the editor's grid, beginning with the selection's original position. To put it another way, you may adjust the selection in "increments" of the grid cell's size.

- Grid

Snaps in place at grid points.

- Vertex

Focuses on the vertex nearest to the mouse pointer.

CHAPTER 6: Objects and Scenes

Using scenes can help you organize your work. A mix file can include many scenes, each of which can interchange objects and materials with the others.

If you are unfamiliar with the principles of Blender's Library and Data System, you should review the instructional page before attempting to manage scenes or create or link libraries.

❖ **Scene**

• Camera

Utilized to choose the camera that is the active camera. Ctrl-Numpad0 may also be used to set the active camera in the 3D Viewport.

• Background Scene

Allows you to use a scene as a backdrop; this is generally useful when you want to focus on animating the foreground without background items interfering with your progress.

You can change any of the components in this scene by selecting it from the Scene data-block menu, even if it has its own animation and physics simulations.

Because they are recursively integrated, Background Scenes can have their own Background Scenes. As a result, you may always contribute to existing scenes by using them as the backdrop for a newly created scene that includes your modifications.

❖ Objects

The geometry of a scene is created by combining one or more components. These things might include simple 2D and 3D forms to fill your scene with models, armatures to animate those models, lights to illuminate it, and cameras to collect images or record videos of everything.

Every Blender object type—such as a mesh, light, curve, camera, etc.—has two components: the object itself and the object data, which is frequently abbreviated to "ObData":

- **Object Types**

- Bend

Mathematically defined objects whose length and curvature may be changed by manipulating them with control handles or control points rather than vertices. View Primitives Curves.

- Mesh

Mesh objects may be extensively altered with Blender's mesh editing features. They consist of vertices, edges, and polygonal faces. See Primitives in Mesh.

- Metaball

Objects made of a mathematical function that defines the 3D volume in which it exists but has neither vertices nor control points. When two or more metaballs are brought together, they merge by gently rounding out the connection, giving the impression of being a single, cohesive item. This is the liquid-like aspect of meta things. Refer to Meta Primitives.

- Surface

Control points are used to alter patches that are specified mathematically. These work well for organic landscapes and basic rounded shapes. Refer to Primitives Surfaces.

- Write something

Construct a two-dimensional text representation.

- Amount

Container for OpenVDB files created using Blender's Fluid Simulator or by other programs.

- Pencil Grease

Things made using brushstroke.

- **Origin of Object**

Every object has an origin. This point's placement determines the three-dimensional position of the item. The origin point is shown by a little circle that appears when an item is selected. When translating, rotating, or scaling an object, the origin point's position is critical. For further information, see Pivot Points. The origin's hue changes depending on the object's selected state.

- In yellow: The object is in motion.
- Orange: The selected object is not active.
- White: The object is not chosen or connected.
- Turquoise: The object is connected.
- Pale turquoise: Though not active, the object is connected and chosen.

■   **Set Origin**

It is possible to move the geometry and object origin in relation to one another and the 3D pointer.

Sort

- From Geometry to Origin

Shifts the model to the origin, causing the object's origin to coincide with its center of mass.

- From Origin to Geometry

Shifts the origin to the object's center.

- From source to 3D Cursor

Shifts the model's origin to the 3D cursor's location.

- From Origin to Center of Mass

Shifts the origin to the model's estimated center of mass (presuming a uniform mesh density).

■   **Selection and Active Object**

Our activities will be focused on certain areas, which will be determined by selection. Selections are made for the observable elements in the current situation. Blender employs complex selection mechanisms. In both Edit and Object modes. Blender distinguishes between two different selection stages.

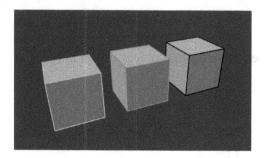

The final (de)selected object in Object Mode is known as the "Active Object" and is highlighted in yellow (the other items are orange). At any given time, there can only be one active item. Several Blender procedures (including linking operations) utilize the active object as a reference. If you already have an item chosen and want to make it the active one, press Shift-LMB again. All other things have been selected. Any number of elements can be selected. Holding Alt while confirming allows you to change a property or perform an operation on all selected objects (bones, sequencer strips).

❖ Collections

A scene may include a huge number of objects: A conventional stage setting includes set pieces, lighting, backdrops, and furniture. Blender helps you organize by grouping like objects together. Unlike parenting, objects can be grouped without creating a transformation connection. You may use collections to simply organize your scene logically or to make it easier to link or attach files or scenes in one click.

▪ Collection Tabs

Convenient property access for the active collection is provided by the collection properties tab.

- **Restriction**

- **Choose-able**

Turns on and off the option to pick items from the 3D Viewport. When you have placed something in the scene and don't want to unintentionally pick it while working on something else, this is helpful.

- **Turn off in Renders**

Enables or disables the collection's render visibility.

- **Withhold**

In the active view layer, objects contained in this collection will produce a holdout or mask.

- **Only Indirect**

Only the shadows and reflections cast by the objects in this collection will directly affect the final image.

- **Instancy**

Offset of instance X, Y, Z

Applies the instanced collections' spatial offset from the origin of the original object.

- **Exporters**

Each collection offers the ability to export to a variety of file formats. These exporters are available worldwide; see Importing and Exporting Files. Nonetheless, this panel makes it easier to export the same asset(s) several times. For example, it may be used to produce and improve the appearance of glTFassets for a game, as well as to create USD assets in a studio pipeline using Blender. The following file types are available; each has documentation for export parameters:

- Alembic
- Universal Scene Description
- Wavefront OBJ
- Stanford PLY
- FBX
- glTF 2.0

- **Line Art**

Usage

The process of loading the collection into line art. If desired, child objects inside the collection have the ability to override this option in Object Properties.

- **Add:** Produce the feature lines for this set.
- **Force-Intersection:** Even when there are things preventing intersection, generate intersection lines.
- **Exclude:** Nothing from this collection will be used to create line art.
- **Only at the Intersection:** Items in the collection don't show their own geometry; instead, they just create junction lines in the scene.
- **Only Occlusion:** Only already-existing feature lines will be obscured by collection objects; their geometry will remain undetectable.
- **Absence of Intersection:** Don't create intersecting lines; just include this collection.

Mask Collection

For the faces in this collection, use a custom intersection mask. The Line Art modifier has the ability to filter lines using intersection masks. For further information, see Collection Masks.

Mask

This mask value will be present at intersections created by this collection.

Intersection priority

Gives this collection an intersection priority value. The item with the greater intersection priority value will contain the intersection line.

❖ View Layers

View layers have visibility settings that are intended to assist in arranging the content that you wish to see or work on.

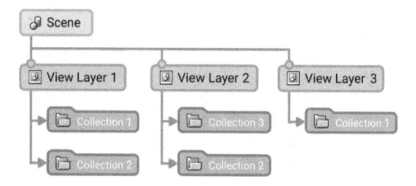

You may change the visibility, selectability, and other aspects of view layers that include references to collections. A view layer can enable any collection, and many view layers can use the same or different collections.

Outliner

In the Outliner, you may modify the view layer collections.

Among other things, you may enable and disable collections as well as temporarily and worldwide conceal them.

CHAPTER 7: Video Editing

Blender is helpful for video editing in addition to modeling and animation. The Video Sequencer (discussed in this chapter) and the Compositor are two practical methods for doing this. You can mix and match several video channels and apply effects to them with Blender's Video Sequencer, a feature-rich video editing system. These effects can be used to create powerful video cuts when paired with Blender's animation features!

❖ Directory Structure

A video production typically blends several different components. They can be separated into three major categories. Images, graphic files (such as logos, charts, etc.), video clips (also known as movies in Blender terminology), and Visual Effects (VFX) such as masks, lens flares, and animation are all considered video files.
• Voice-over, music, recorded dialogue, and Sound Effects (SFX) such as swooshes and background noise are all included in audio files.

• Project files consist of storyboards and scripts for documentation, mix files, backups, and partial render outputs.

Modify Your Work

There isn't a single video editing recommended practice that applies to every circumstance. Although there are certainly many particular use cases, such as editing educational videos and producing wedding films, there is broad agreement that four basic processes should be separated.

- **Montage**

The technique of assembling various text, audio, video, and effects elements into a coherent whole is called montage. In the 1910s and 1920s, Russian filmmaker Lev Kuleshov was the first to demonstrate the benefits of montage. Viewers understand two consecutive images together more meaningfully than they do a single image alone, according to the well-known Kuleshov effect (for a beautiful example, check out the Wikipedia article).

- **Editing**

Move

- Offset of the Start Frame

By clicking LMB on the strip's left handle, you may select the Start Frame Offset for that particular strip. You can also change the start frame inside the strip by dragging it to the left or right while holding down the mouse button or by hitting G. The frame number indicator underneath it indicates the start of the strip.

- Offset of the End Frame

Click LMB on the right handle of the strip to select its End Frame. Then you can move the mouse while holding down the mouse button (or hit G) to adjust the strip's final frame. The frame number label above it displays the strip's last frame.

- Expand or Shift Out of the Current Frame

You may use the E key to interact with the strips when you have selected more than one. This functions similarly to moving and may be used to increase (or decrease) time around the current frame.

All selected strip handles can be changed to the "mouse side" of the indicator to change the length of the strips at the current frame.

- Content of the Slip Strip

With the Slip tool, you can move the contents of a strip without moving the strip itself.

- Removing Gaps

Regardless of whether the strips are selected or locked, remove the blank frames that appear in the present frame and the initial strip to the left.

CHAPTER 8: Physics

Blender 4.3 physics framework allows you to mimic a wide range of physical phenomena that occur in the actual world. Numerous static and dynamic effects may be created with these systems, such as:

- Flocks, grass, and hair

- Rainfall

- Dust and smoke

- Water

- Cloth

- Jelly etc.

❖ **Rigid Body**

The rigid body simulation may be used to model the motion of solid objects. It changes an object's orientation and location without   distorting   it.

Compared to the other simulations, Blender's stiff body simulation has a closer interaction with the animation system. Therefore, much as regular objects, rigid bodies may be used in parent-child relationships, animation constraints, and drivers.

- **Creating a Rigid Body**

There can only be mesh objects in a rigid body simulation. To create stiff bodies, use the stiff Body button in the Properties' Physics tab under the Object ‣ Rigid Body menu – Add Active/Add Passive.

There are two types of rigid bodies: active and passive. Active bodies are dynamically simulated, whereas passive bodies remain motionless. Both types may be controlled by the animation system when the animated option is selected.

Throughout the simulation, the rigid body system will take precedence over the orientation and position of dynamic rigid body items. Note that the rigid body simulation acts more like a constraint because the objects' position and rotation don't change. The rigid body transformations are implemented using the implement Object Transform operator.

The scale of the rigid body item has an impact on the simulation, even if it is always controlled by the animation system.

The object's rigid body physics can be removed using the Object

Rigid Body option or the Rigid Body button on the Properties' Physics   tab.

- **Working with Rigid Body**

The stiff Body object menu provides access to many object operators that may be used to work with stiff bodies. These operators include functions to add and remove rigid bodies, modify the properties of rigid bodies, and apply rigid body restrictions.

- **Rigid Body World**

All of the rigid bodies in this paradigm have configurations that are shared by a group of rigid body objects called the Rigid Body World.

A collection of items known as "Rigid Body World" is automatically created when an object is subjected to rigid body physics. when the body is stiff toward this group. When you distribute the physics to an item using the Collections panel, several stiff Body World Collections are created and the object's stiff body is immediately added.

Only rigid body objects and limitations that are included in the collection set in the Collections field of the Rigid Body World panel in the Scene tab are taken into account by the simulation.

- **Rigid Body Constraint**

Two rigid bodies are joined by rigid body joints, sometimes referred to as restrictions. The physics constraints are meant to be attached to a blank object. The constraint can be used to guide the fields of the two physics-enabled objects it will bind. The empty object provides the constraint with a location and an axis, in contrast to the two constrained things. A set of axes and a location are indicated by the position of the entity having the physics constraint on each of the two constrained items.

For the duration of the animation, the two anchor points' orientation and location—which are established at the beginning of the animation—remain fixed in the local coordinate system of the object. The constraint anchor tracks the object's journey even while the objects are allowed to move away from it. If this feature seems restricted, think about using several objects with a non-physics kid of limitation and animating the relative positioning of the kid.

❖ Physics Menu

Furthermore, you may apply a stiff body constraint to any of the two constrained objects by using the stiff Body Constraint button on the Physics tab in the Properties. This constraint depends on a number of things, including the item's rotation and location. No empty objects are created for the limitation in this way. The empty object's function is assumed by this object. The constrained object may subsequently be set to a passive type to enhance constraint driving.

The Properties of the chosen empty object or one of the two constrained objects with the built constraint in the panel of the Physics tab's Rigid Body Constraint display additional options.

▪ Types of Constraint

• Fixed

This restriction causes the two objects to move in tandem. Since there is some slop in the physics system, the objects do not move with the same stiffness as if they were all a part of the same mesh.

• Hinge

One degree of flexibility between two things is allowed by the hinge. There are strong limitations on translation. The item with the Physics constraint, usually an empty object different from the two objects being linked, may rotate along its Z axis. You may modify the axis and anchor of the hinge by changing the position and rotation of the object that contains the constraint.

The Hinge is a special single-axis rotating limitation that uses the Z axis rather than the X axis. If your hinge isn't functioning properly, look at your other limits to see if they may be the cause of the problem.

- **Point**

The objects are connected by a point bearing, which allows rotation around the location of the constraint object but not relative translation. The constraint object will identify the two places on the two constrained objects, and the physics engine will try to make sure that they coincide.

- **Slider**

The Slider constraint allows relative translation along the X axis of the constraint object, but not relative rotation or translation along other axes.

- **Piston**

Translation along the constraint object's X axis is made possible using a piston. Additionally, it permits rotation around the constraint object's X axis. It is similar to combining the freedoms of a hinge and a slider, neither of which is particularly free on its own.

- **Generic**

There are many different parameters for the generic constraint.

The restrictions on the X, Y, and Z axes can be used to limit the amount of translation between the objects. Clamping the min/max to zero yields the same result as the point constraint.

When the relative rotation is limited to zero, the objects stay in alignment. Combining an absolute rotation with a translation clamp would behave similarly to the Fixed constraint.

Throughout the simulation, every parameter that has a nonzero spread added to it will fluctuate within that range.

- **Generic Spring**

The generic spring constraint adds specific spring parameters for the X, Y, and Z axes to all the options available on the generic constraint. The objects move as if they are tied to the restricting object by a spring when the spring is utilized alone. This is a little too flexible for most uses, and it is preferable to add rotation or translation restrictions.

When the damping on the springs is set to 1, the spring pressures cannot realign the anchor points, which causes unusual behavior. If your springs are acting oddly, check the damping.

- **Motor**

The motor constraint causes two items to be rotated and/or translated. It can force two things apart or together. It can drive fundamental rotation and translation, but unlike a screw, it won't be constrained because translation may be limited by other physical rules without impacting rotation.

The rotation axis is the object that contains the X axis of the constraint. In contrast, the Z axis is used by the hinge. Since the Motor is vulnerable to confusing disturbances when there is no equivalent hinge restriction, it is extremely crucial to align the axes. If the hinge is obstructing the motor's operation, the motor will seem to have no effect if it is not correctly aligned.

- **Tips**

The Animated checkbox on the Rigid Body panel on the Physics header in the Properties should be closely inspected, just as with any other physics-enabled object. Not ticking the Animated box while using the keyframe animation for an inactive physics object is a typical error. Disappointment will result from the item moving but the physics engine acting as though the Passive is still in its initial position.

❖ Animation

The most widely used technique involves keyframe animating an Active Physics object's position or spin in addition to the animated checkbox. When a curve in the animated property becomes disabled, the physics engine takes over based on the object's rotation, velocity, and last known position.

A wide variety of interesting results might be obtained by animating the strengths of various elements (such as a hinge's limitations, a motor's goal velocity, etc.).

Because the physics engine is attempting to align two objects that are often far out of alignment, enabling a limitation during a physics simulation often results in spectacular effects. Frequently, the affected objects gain enough momentum to spring out of the frame.

It is possible to bake rigid body dynamics to standard keyframes by selecting the Bake to Keyframes option from the Object ▸ Rigid Body menu.

- **Simulation Stability**

The easiest way to boost simulation stability is to increase steps per second. However, caution must be exercised because adding too many steps might cause problems and further degrade the simulation's stability (if you need more than 1000 steps, you should examine other techniques to boost stability).

Strengthening constraints and increasing object stacking stability are two benefits of increasing the number of solver iterations. Because they are fragile at the moment, little things should be avoided. Ideally, objects should be at least 20 centimeters in diameter. Although it is generally not recommended, if it is still necessary, setting the collision margin to 0 can help small objects behave more naturally.

When objects are small or move fast, they can pass through each other. In addition to the previously mentioned guidance, it is advisable to refrain from using mesh forms in this situation. Things may flow through mesh shapes more easily since they are composed of individual triangles rather than having any real thickness. To give them some thickness, you may raise the collision margin.

❖ **Cloth**

Simulating fabric is one of the most challenging aspects of computer graphics. Although it seems simple and is sometimes taken for granted in real life, there are many complex internal and external interactions involved. Usually, fabric is represented as 2D mesh to mimic real-world objects such as textiles, banners, and flags. However, 3D objects like teddy bears, balls, pillows, and balloons may also be simulated with cloth.

In addition to a general aerodynamic model, you may customize how fabric interacts with and is affected by the wind, other moving objects, and other variables.

Once fabric physics has been applied to a mesh, a fabric Modification will be added to the object's modifier stack. Therefore, given its role as a modifier, it can react with other modifiers such as Armature and Smooth. In these cases, the modifier stack order is used to determine the final mesh shape. For example, you should smooth the material when the modifier calculates the shape of the fabric.

Use the Cloth Modifier to lock in or freeze the mesh's shape at that frame. The modifier is eliminated as a result. For example, you might place a flat cloth over a table, run the simulation, and then apply the adjustment. In this sense, you are effectively saving yourself by using the simulator.

Because the simulation's output is cached, once the shape of the mesh has been established for a certain animation frame, it is not necessary to calculate it again. If you alter the simulation, you have total control over clearing the cache and restarting the experiment. When the simulation runs for the first time, it does so automatically without the need for baking or further processes.

You may continue working while the simulation is running since the shape of the fabric is automatically determined at each frame and is done in the background. It is CPU-intensive, though, because the complexity of the simulation and the power of your PC determine how much CPU is needed to compute the mesh and how much latency is conceivable.

- **Workflow**

When dealing with cloth, a common procedure is to:

- Use the Cloth object as a basic form to begin with.
- In the Properties, under the Physics tab, label the item as "cloth."
- Create a model of any extra deflection components that may touch the fabric. In the modifier stack, make sure the Deflection modification is applied after any other mesh-deforming modifiers.
- Apply materials and textures, illuminate the fabric, and, if desired, do UV unwrapping.
- If you like, add some particles to the object, such as steam coming from the surface.
- To obtain the intended results, run the simulation and make the required modifications. The playback controls in the Timeline editor are excellent for this stage.
- You have the option to age the mesh to a certain point throughout the simulation in order to obtain a new default starting shape.
- Make minor modifications frame by frame to repair any rips in the mesh.

❖ **Fluid**

  ▪ **Gas Simulations**

Gas or smoke simulations can be used to model airborne mixes of gases, liquid particles, and solids, including smoke, within the context of the fluids system. It depicts the density, heat, and velocity of various other fluids or suspended particles, like smoke, and creates dynamic Voxel textures that may be utilized for rendering. It also simulates the fluid movement of air. A mesh object or particle system emits gasses or smoke inside a domain. The movement of smoke is controlled by the domain's airflow, which is influenced by Effector objects. Smoke will also be affected by the environment's gravity and force fields. Airflow in the domain can affect other physics models through the Fluid Flow force field.

> ➢ **Liquid Simulations**

Fluid physics simulates the physical properties of liquids, especially water. When creating a scene in Blender, you may identify certain objects to be a part of the flowing simulation. A fluid simulation requires a domain that defines the space that the simulation takes up. Under the domain settings, you may set the simulation's global parameters, such as gravity and viscosity.

- • **Settings**

The domain object contains the whole simulation. Fluid simulations cannot leave the domain; depending on the settings, they will either smash against the edge or disappear.

Keep in mind that higher resolutions and longer bake times are needed for bigger domains. It should be just large enough to accommodate the simulation without making computations too laborious.

To create a domain, add a cube and drag it about until it entirely encloses the area where you want the simulation to take place. Translation, rotation, and scaling are all allowed. To make it a fluid domain, choose Domain as the fluid type after selecting Fluid under the Properties ‣ Physics tab.

- **Flow**

Use fluid flow types to add or withdraw fluid from a domain object. A flow object needs to be contained inside the domain's Bounding Box in order to operate.

To apply Fluid physics to any mesh object and designate it as a Flow object, click Fluid under Properties ‣ Physics. Next, select Flow as the fluid type. You should now have access to a fluid flow origin object that has been predefined.

CHAPTER 9: Painting and Sculpting

The brush editing technique is more adaptable in painting and sculpting. This may be done in a number of ways, each serving a different purpose.

❖ Brush

The brush is the main tool used in any painting or sculpting mode. Clicking and dragging in the 3D Viewport will create a stroke and apply an effect based on the brush parameters.

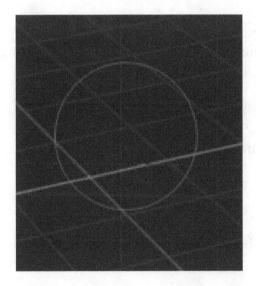

Brush Settings

The most popular keys for adjusting the brush are these ones.

- Use the F brush size.
- Brush strength setting Shift + F.
- Ctrl + F to adjust the brush's weight and rotate its texture.

After tapping these keys, you may change the value interactively or by inputting numbers. Move the mouse right or left to further change the value with precision (Shift) and/or snapping (Ctrl) enabled. Finally, confirm (LMB, Return) or cancel (RMB, Esc). You may also change the direction or effect of the brush by holding down Ctrl.

- **Stroke**

The behavior of the painted or sculpted stroke is defined by the stroke parameters. Over the stroke, any additional brush behavior or effect is added.

Stroke Methods

Specifies how the paint is applied on the canvas using brushstrokes.

- **Drag Point:**

Just leaves one dab, which may be moved with a drag, on the canvas.

- **Distance:**

Restricts the amount of brush work to the distance indicated by the brush radius %.

- **Dots:**

Paint every mouse movement step. This is dependent on the stroke speed rather than how far apart they are from one another. This implies that greater cumulative strength will be used with a slower stroke.

- **Area:**

Produces brush strokes in the form of a string of dots, the spacing of which is controlled by the Spacing parameter.

- **Airbrush:**

Depending on the Rate option, the brush's flow will continue as long as the mouse click is held (spray).

- **From Edge to Edge:**

The brush's position and orientation are indicated by a two-point circle. One point is created by the initial click, and the second point, which is opposite the first, is created by dragging.

- **Curve:**

Uses a Bézier curve to define the stroke curve (dabs are spaced based on spacing). Blender stores this Bézier curve as a "Paint Curve" data-block.

- **Line:**

To define a line in screen space, click and drag. Like space strokes, spacing is used to separate the line dabs. The line stroke is limited to 45 degree increments while using Alt.

- **Stabilize Stroke**

Maintain stability Stroke adds a soft curve to the stroke's path and makes it follow the cursor. This may be enabled by pressing Shift S or by checking the box in the header.

- Radius

Minimum separation required before the stroke resumes from the previous position.

- Factor

Higher values of this smooth factor provide smoother strokes, but the sketching experience is still similar to tugging the stroke.

- **Visibility and Selection**

Sometimes, painting on the necessary vertices in a complex model might be challenging. Assume you wish to paint a small area of the mesh while leaving the remainder bare. In this case, "selection masking" is helpful. When this mode is enabled, a brush will only paint on the selected faces or vertices.

Selection masking is superior to the normal paint method in the following ways:

- Even when modifiers are engaged, the original mesh boundaries remain visible.
- Instead of going into Edit Mode, you may choose and deselect faces.

Masking Vertex Selection

In this mode, you may choose one or more vertices and then paint only on those vertices. All unselected vertices are protected against accidental changes.

Face Selection Masking

Similar to vertex selection masking, face selection masking lets you pick faces and restrict the paintbrush to specific faces.

Unhide or Hide Faces

In Edit Mode, you may also hide some faces by using the keyboard shortcut H. The faces that are still visible can then be painted over. Finally, you may uncover the concealed faces again by pressing Alt-H.

Unhide or Hide Vertices

Only a subset of faces may be selectively hidden in vertex mask selection mode. However, the selection changes as you change the selection modes. Therefore, a common ploy is to:

- To convert the selection to faces, go to the Face selection mask mode.
- Next, hone your choices or simply conceal the faces.
- Return to the mask mode for Vertex Selection.

Vertices that belong to visible faces will always be visible thanks to hiding faces.

❖ **Sculpting**

Although you may alter a model's appearance in both Sculpt Mode and Edit Mode, they work very differently. First, instead of editing individual parts of the model, such as faces, edges, and vertices, brushes are used to edit a specific area of the model.

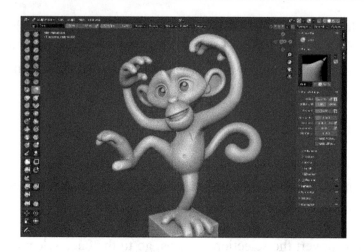

To enter Sculpt Mode, press Ctrl + Tab. Alternatively, you may use the mode menu in the 3D Viewport header or the pie menu. Once you are in Sculpt Mode, the Toolbar and Tool Settings in the 3D Viewport will change to panels that are only available in Sculpt Mode. The pointer will transform to a circle as the brush size is altered.

- **The Brush**

Sculpt Mode is easily recognized by the appearance and behavior of the brush. All other brush settings are still relevant even if the sculpting brush is displayed in three dimensions. This means that the brush will follow the curvature of the surface if the radius is aligned with the topological Normal. The inner ring of the brush cursor may be used to see the strength of the brush.

The brush is frequently applied to other tools on the toolbar to enhance tool visibility. For example, the Box Trim and Lasso Trim tools allow you to control the depth of geometry removal or insertion by adjusting the current brush radius.

Common Brushes

Although there are many more brushes available, these are the ones that are most frequently used for sculpting. More on how to use the sculpting brushes in the Toolbar. Clay Strips: Prior to further honing them, this brush is used to create volumes and block out huge forms;

- Grab: For general sculpting, this brush pushes geometry across the screen.
- Smooth: To eliminate noise or flatten forms, this brush shrinks and smoothes surfaces.
- Draw: This brush adds and subtracts on surfaces; it may be tailored with different textures and stroke patterns to create a variety of effects.
- Scratch: For vigorous smoothing or hard surface sculpting, this brush adds and fills surfaces.
- Inflate: This brush is very helpful for regulating the thickness of cylindrical forms since it may expand or compress volumes or surfaces.
- Draw Sharp: This brush works well for creating wrinkles, cracks, and other sharp edges since it has a considerably sharper falloff than Draw.
- Crease: A cross between the Draw and Pinch brushes. good for creating precise creases or for adding more shine to creases that already present.
- Snake Hook: This brush will dynamically release pressure and pick up geometry as it strokes, despite operating identically to Grab. The dragged geometry follows the angle of the stroke, which facilitates drawing geometry out. It works best when used with Dyntopo.

- **Gesture Tools**

Sculpt mode offers a set of tools that perform actions to a specified sketched region in addition to brushes and filters. Blender's selection tools, such box and lasso selection, are similar to these capabilities.

Instead than providing a selection of pieces to be changed later, these tools instantly change the underlying geometry.

Polyline Gestures

A point is placed in the viewport when you click. A new point in the polygon is formed each time LMB is pushed. The selection box closes when you hit Return or LMB on the starting point.

Lasso Gestures

When you drag, a freeform region is created that follows the cursor that is determined by the locations of the LMB presses and releases.

Box Gestures

The location of where LMB was pushed and released define a rectangular region that is created by dragging.

Line Gestures

A line is made by dragging. Everything on the highlighted side of the line is impacted by the ensuing action. The region that is being operated upon extends beyond the viewpoint in both directions.

- **Masking, Face Set and Visibility**

Visibility Control

Parts of the mesh can be hidden in Sculpt Mode. Because ugly faces don't move, it's easier to isolate the parts you want to focus on. Hide geometry also improves viewport performance. The hiding capability is shared by all modes except Object Mode; faces that are hidden or visible in one mode will likewise be concealed in other modes.

Sculpt Mode primarily uses Masks and Face Sets to control mesh visibility and which faces may be changed at the present, as opposed to other painting modes that employ Selection Masking. One exception is the Clipping Region, which can be used in any mode.

The most often used keyboard shortcuts are H to hide the face set under the pointer and Shift-H to isolate the face set beneath the cursor (or display everything).

You can also invert visibility and make everything visible by using the Alt + W pie menu.

The Hide Gesture Tools can also be used to change visibility.

Masks

A mask controls the vertices of the mesh that are impacted by painting and sculpting. For example, the mask may be created and altered using the Mask by Color and Mask Gesture Tools.

The sculpt-mask Attributes are used internally to store masks.

Invert and Clear

There are several differences between the mental model used for selecting in other modes and the one utilized for mask creation. For example, instead of supplementing a mask, Shift + LMB is used to achieve smoothness.

Masking is conceptually the reverse of selection in that masked vertices are immutable. On the other hand, certain vertices are editable.

Instead, you nearly always use Ctrl + LMB to remove a mask and LMB to apply it to the one that already exists. Therefore, if you wish to alter the masked surfaces, you will have to utilize the Invert operator. The best method is to clear the mask first, then reverse it if you want to cover everything that is visible.

Both of these operators may be quickly accessed via the A pie menu.

Face Sets

Face sets, which organize your mesh into different colored faces, may quickly hide or reveal your mesh as previously said. They may also be used to quickly make masks using the Mask Expand. Additionally, Face Set Expand allows you to create, edit, and join face sets.

Additional options are available in the Alt + W pie menu. Otherwise, Face Sets may be created and altered with the Draw Face Sets brush and Mask Gesture Tools. They may also be changed using the edit Face Set tool.

Auto Masking

Auto-masking is another fast way to simply change specific geometry without having to manually create a new mask or conceal geometry. When used with face sets, this function performs quite effectively.

- **Filters**

Filters are tools that provide a different approach to sculpting by influencing any visible and unmasked vertices, as they are independent of a brush radius.

By clicking and dragging from left to right, you may change the strength. The location of the cursor can be used to selectively affect specific areas if auto-masking is enabled.

A variety of brush styles are also available as filter types. This allows for the simultaneous coloring, smoothing, or coating of a sizable section of the mesh with cloth simulation.

- **Transforming**

You can move, rotate, and scale using transform tools in Sculpt Mode as well, although it differs greatly from other modes. The pivot point in Sculpt Mode can be manually set with Shift-RMB or automatically set using Mask Expand. This ensures that the pivot point may be positioned more freely and travels continuously with the changed shape. Instead of constantly utilizing the transform tools, you may opt to always have access to the viewport gizmos by turning them on.

- **Painting**

Additionally, you may use Color Attributes, such as Vertex Colors in Sculpt Mode, to paint your geometry. This ensures that the most frequently performed operations within the sculpting workflow are included in the same mode, preventing unnecessary mode change.

Masking, filters, and face sets are examples of other sculpt mode aspects that may be used with painting tools. The Paint and Smear brushes, the Color Filter, and the Mask by Color tool are the only painting tools accessible in Sculpt Mode.

As with other brushes, Shift may be used for smoothing. Instead, when using brushes to paint, it will blur the colors inside the brush radius.

- **Adaptive Resolution**

Blender requires sufficient geometry for sculpting in order to produce accurate and consistent results. Instead of starting with a sharply divided mesh, dynamically add geometry using one of the following adaptive sculpting approaches.

- **Voxel Remeshing**

By rebuilding the geometry using "voxel remeshing," a perfectly even distributed topology is produced. Depending on the chosen voxel size, this will provide a resolution that is either lower or greater.

This technique is very effective at blocking the original shape of an object. Additionally, it has the advantage of removing any overlapping geometry, which creates a manifold volume. A re-projected mask, face settings, and color will all be included in the remeshed output.

or attributes that are currently in use. Depending on the hardware being utilized, large vertex counts should still be possible with this method.

- **Dyntopo**

Dynamic topology, or Dyntopo, is a dynamic tessellation sculpting method that automatically adds and subtracts structure underneath the brush.

Unlike the Voxel Remesher, this enables the construction of complex structures without requiring topology or resolution considerations. It also makes it possible to define a different resolution when necessary. Much more complex foundation mesh sculpting is particularly useful with this technique. Slower performance and limited compatibility with some sculpt mode features are the disadvantages of this approach. Custom attributes like Face Sets, UV Maps, and Color properties are also lost or altered while using Dyntopo.

This feature has the same shortcuts as voxel remeshing when it is enabled. If Constant Detail is being used, define the resolution with R and then flood fill it with Ctrl + R.

- **Multi-resolution**

The Multi-resolution Modifier may be used for subdivision-based modeling. This means that the object will be divided similarly to the Subdivision Surface Modifier, except that the subdivisions can be freely sculpted for really fine details.

Because it can be done at several resolutions, this method has the benefit of being able to be utilized to sculpt at any subdivision level. This allows details to be added at a much higher resolution for rendering and sculpting, while displaying lesser resolutions for increased viewport efficiency. It also allows sculpting at any time at lower resolutions for more detailed modifications.

You may, for instance, sculpt general proportions in subdivision level 1, add high resolution details in level 4, and then return to subdivision 1 to further fix the shape. One disadvantage is that you could have some mesh distortions because the topology is not dynamic like voxel remeshing and dyntopo. Furthermore, the topology should not be changed after a subdivision has been created as this will taint the subdivision data.

- **Cloth Sculpting**

Instead of manually sculpting fabric or creating complex physics simulation settings, there are a number of tools accessible in sculpt mode that offer a simpler fabric physics simulation.

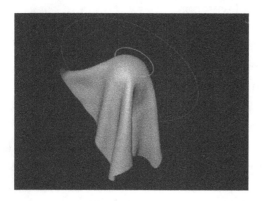

There are several advantages to this, but it's especially useful for making foundation mesh and larger folds and drapes for clothing. Detailing is possible, but the slower performance and diminished fabric mechanics on high resolution models could not provide the intended results.

The resolution of the topology largely determines the size of the folds and the amount of complexity of the simulation. Therefore, having a uniformly distributed ideal topology is essential. There are several sculpting options available, such as masked vertices being pinned in the simulation. The borders of the auto-masked face set provide as another example. The sculpt mode gravity factor is also applied by the textile physics.

The main brushes and tools for this feature are the fabric Brush and Cloth Filter, although by modifying their brush parameters, additional transform brushes like Pose and Boundary may also be used for fabric sculpting.

❖ **Texture Paint**

A UV texture is an image, sequence, or movie that is used to color the surface of a mesh. The UV texture is mapped to the model using one or more UV maps. There are three methods to identify the image that the UV texture uses:

- • Any image editing program may be used to create a picture. Import the image into the Image Editor after selecting the UV texture. Blender will then use the texture's UV map to apply the colors to the mesh's faces.
  • To add color to the mesh's faces, paint a flat image over the UV map of the currently selected UV texture in the picture   editor.
  • Blender will use the currently selected UV map to update the UV texture after the object has been painted in the 3D Viewport (as detailed below).

• Blender's built-in Texture Paint mode is specifically designed to make it easy and quick to modify UV textures and images in the Image Editor or 3D Viewport. Since a UV texture is only an image meant for a particular usage, you may make it using any external paint program, such GIMP or Krita. Since a mesh may have layers of UV textures, it may have several pictures that color it. However, each UV texture has a single image.

Texture Paint may be used in a 3D viewport or in the Image Editor. You may paint directly on the mesh by projecting into the 3D Viewport's UVs when in Texture Paint Mode.

- **Texture preview**

If, in your scene, your texture is already being used to color, bump map, displace, alpha-transparent, etc. on a model's surface (or, to put it more technically, is mapped to some aspect of a texture via a texture channel using UV as a map input), you can see the effects of your painting as you paint.

To do this, set up two nearby regions, one with the Texture Shading option in the 3D Viewport selected and the other with the Image Editor loaded. To see the UV-mapped object on the loaded image, set the 3D Viewport. This technique, called "bump mapping," creates the illusion of a rough surface on a flat region by mapping the texture being painted in the picture to the right to the "Normal" attribute and using a grayscale image. See Texture Mapping Output for more information on bump mapping.

- **Mask**

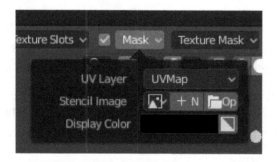

Stencil Mask

To better define the masked surfaces, apply a texture to the picture. Mask surfaces can be defined using the Mask brush, but painting won't change them. You may disable the mask by checking the box in the header.
Mask   for   Cavities

Depending on the mesh selections, cavity masking means that if the mesh surface has a hill or a hollow, the brushes will be covered. Cavity uses a vertex-based method.

❖ **Vertex Painting**

By changing the color of vertices rather than textures, vertex painting is a relatively simple technique for adding color to an object. Vertex Painting preserves color information as a Color Attribute that may be used by a number of render engines. You may change the color properties using the pallette pop-over that is situated in the middle of the header.

When a vertex is painted according to the brush's specifications, its color changes. The color of all visible planes and edges connected to the vertex is then altered by applying a gradient to the color of the other connected vertices. Remember, faces that are veiled do not lose their color.

▪ **Editing**

• **Vertex Dirty Color**

Create a gradient dirt map according to cavity (Paint ‣ Dirty Vertex Colors).

• **Saturation/Hue/Value**

Modify the chosen vertices' HSV values (Paint ›
Saturation/Hue/Value).

- **Vertex Smooth Color**

Colors that are smooth across vertices (Paint › Smooth Vertex
Colors)

- **Vertex Color from Weight**

Converts the colors of the active weight to grayscale (Paint ›
Vertex Color from Weight).

- **Contrast and Brightness**

Modify the chosen vertices' contrast and brightness (Paint ›
Contrast/Brightness).

- ❖ **Weight Paint**

Vertex groups can have a very high number of connected vertices
and, consequently, a large number of weights (one weight per
assigned vertex). Weight painting is a very natural way to save a
lot of weight information.
Primarily used for rigging meshes, the vertex groups indicate the
relative bone effects on the mesh. But we also use it to regulate
particle emission, hair density, shape keys, and a number of
modifiers.
You may enter Weight Paint Mode by using the Ctrl-Tab mode
option. The selected mesh object seems considerably dimmed and
in a rainbow of hues. The color indicates the weights given to each
vertex in the active vertex group. By default, blue denotes
unweighted and red denotes fully weighted.

You may give the object's vertices weights by painting on it with weight brushes. When painting on a mesh, weights are instantly applied to the active vertex group (if a new vertex group is required,   a   new   one   is   created).

You may manage Vertex Groups using the pallette pop-over in the middle of the header.

- **The Color Code for Weighting**

Weights are represented by a gradient with a cold/hot color scheme. Areas with weights close to 0.0, or low value, are displayed as blue (cool), and those with weights close to 1.0, or high value, are displayed as red (hot). The colors blue, green, yellow, orange, and red are also used to depict all intermediate values as a rainbow.

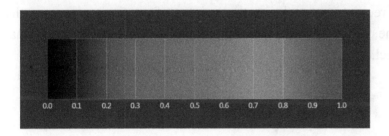

In addition to the color system just discussed, Blender provides an extra visual notation (optional) for unreferenced vertices, which is represented by the color black. This allows you to view the referred sections (represented by cold/hot colors) and the unreferenced portions (represented by black) at the same time. This is particularly practical when looking for weighting errors.

- **Weight Normalized Workflow**

To be used for tasks like deformation, weights frequently need to be normalized such that all of the deforming weights applied to a single vertex add up to one. It is theoretically not necessary to ensure that weights are normalized prior to painting because Blender's Armature modifier handles this automatically. Working with normalized weights provides certain advantages despite being more complicated, such as making it possible to utilize tools designed specifically for this purpose and eliminating the requirement to know the weights of previous groups on the same vertex in order to comprehend the present group's final effect.

- **Vertex Group Uses**

- **Bones Vertex Group**

This is one of the main uses for weight painting. Even while Blender can create the weights for you (see the section on skinning), you may want to modify or even create your own, particularly for joints.

The steps involved are as follows:

- Using Ctrl + Tab, choose the armature and put it in Pose Mode.

- Verify that the topbar's Edit ‣ Lock Object Modes option is not selected.
- After choosing the mesh, enter Weight Paint Mode.
- Verify that the 3D Viewport's header has Bone Selection checked.
- Use Alt-LMB (or Shift-Ctrl-LMB) to choose a bone. This will cause the mesh to display the bone's current weights and activate its vertex group.
- Use LMB to paint weights for the bone.

For any bone that doesn't have a vertex group when you start painting, Blender will create one for you.

If your mesh and armature are symmetrical, you may use Mirror Vertex Groups to automatically create vertex groups and weights for the other side.

www.ingramcontent.com/pod-product-compliance
Lightning Source LLC
Chambersburg PA
CBHW071003050326
40689CB00014B/3475